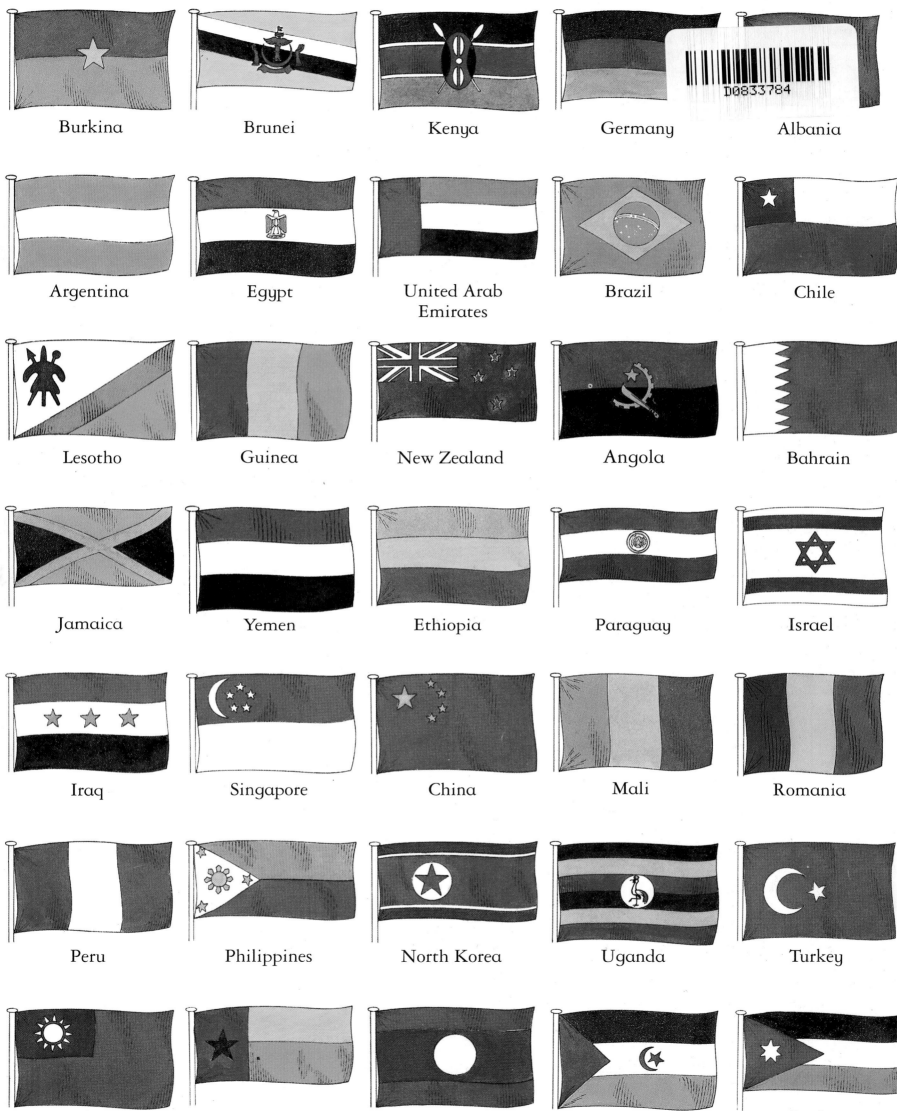

Burkina	Brunei	Kenya	Germany	Albania
Argentina	Egypt	United Arab Emirates	Brazil	Chile
Lesotho	Guinea	New Zealand	Angola	Bahrain
Jamaica	Yemen	Ethiopia	Paraguay	Israel
Iraq	Singapore	China	Mali	Romania
Peru	Philippines	North Korea	Uganda	Turkey
Taiwan	Guinea-Bissau	Laos	Western Sahara	Jordan

My First Atlas

Written by
Bill Boyle

Illustrated by
Dave Hopkins

DK

DORLING KINDERSLEY
London • New York • Stuttgart

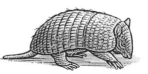

DK

A Dorling Kindersley Book

Note to Parents

My First Atlas has been specially designed to introduce young children to the countries and continents of the world and to the language of maps. By looking at the colourful picture maps and photographs, children will develop an understanding of the different regions of the world and their distinctive features. For each region, children will find out whether the climate is hot or cold, where the rivers or mountains are, where people live and work, the crops that farmers grow, and the plants and animals that inhabit the area. These features will enable children to build a wider view of the world by comparing the differences between countries.

Each double page offers many topics for discussion. Open-ended questions will stimulate children to talk about and use each picture map and help them to locate places in the world. A journey line is marked in red across each map. As children trace each imaginary journey, they will gain information about what they might see on a visit to each part of the world. The journey box on each map estimates the time it would take to travel the route by plane or car, introducing children to a sense of scale and distance.

The introductory section of this book aims to explain to children what maps are, and how and why we use them. Maps and the information they contain are starting points in a child's explorations. *My First Atlas* is the ideal book to encourage children to want to find out more about our amazing planet.

Bill Boyle   Author

Project Editors Monica Byles,
Fran Jones
Art Editor Peter Radcliffe
Managing Editor Jane Yorke

Managing Art Editor Chris Scollen
Production Ruth Cobb
Cartographic Research Roger Bullen
Picture Research Catherine O'Rourke

Editor's Note
Only the national flag of each country is shown on the endpapers of this book.

First published in Great Britain in 1994
by Dorling Kindersley Limited,
9 Henrietta Street, London WC2E 8PS
Copyright © 1994 Dorling Kindersley Limited, London

A CIP catalogue record for this book is available from the British Library.

ISBN 0-7513-5201-2

Reproduced by Classicscan, Singapore
Printed and bound in Italy by L.E.G.O.

Contents

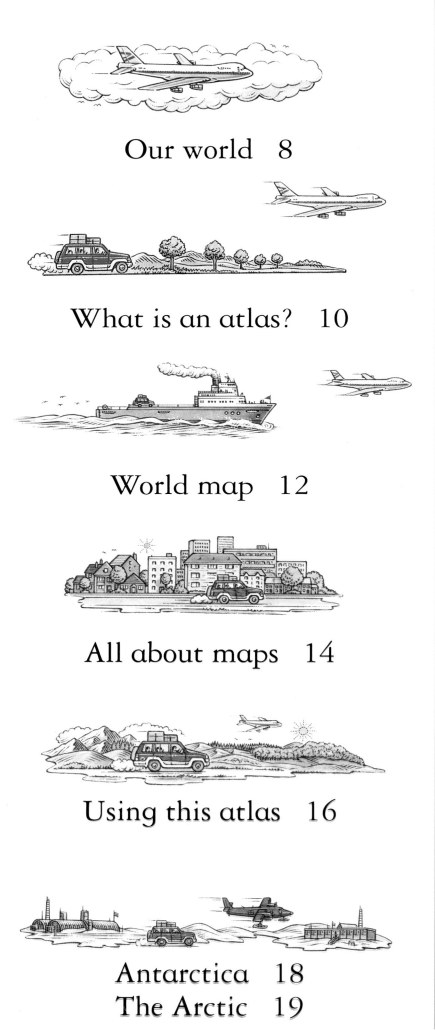

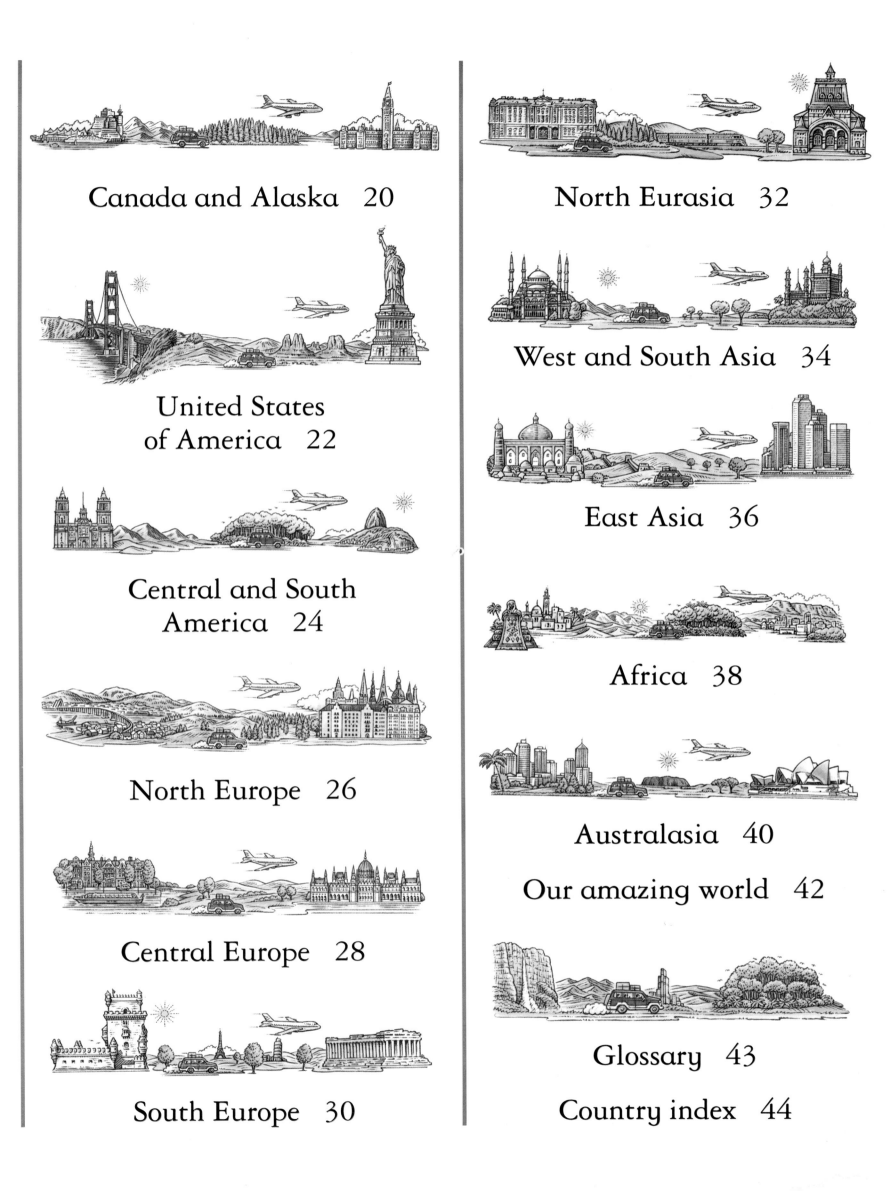

Our world

We live on a planet called the Earth, which is a huge ball of rock, floating in space. The Earth, our world, is always turning, but we cannot feel it moving.

Our world looks flat from the ground or from the air, but in fact it is round. We know this because people have travelled into space and taken photographs of our planet.

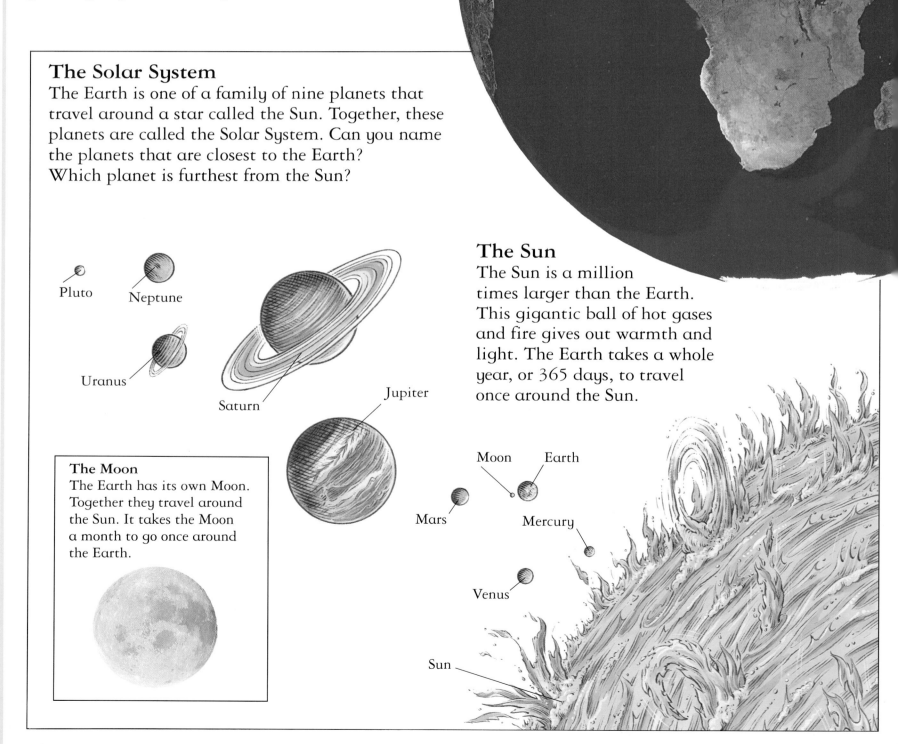

The Solar System

The Earth is one of a family of nine planets that travel around a star called the Sun. Together, these planets are called the Solar System. Can you name the planets that are closest to the Earth? Which planet is furthest from the Sun?

Pluto

Neptune

Uranus

Saturn

Jupiter

The Sun

The Sun is a million times larger than the Earth. This gigantic ball of hot gases and fire gives out warmth and light. The Earth takes a whole year, or 365 days, to travel once around the Sun.

Moon   Earth

Mars

Mercury

Venus

The Moon

The Earth has its own Moon. Together they travel around the Sun. It takes the Moon a month to go once around the Earth.

Sun

The Earth in space

This is a space satellite photograph of the Earth. It shows that most of the planet is covered in sea. Look closely at the land. Can you tell where there are rivers, lakes, or mountains?

Space satellite
A space satellite is a machine that travels in outer space, collecting and sending information to our planet.

Looking at the Earth

The Earth is so large that you can only see its round shape from far out in space. From this distance, you can only recognize the shapes of the land and the sea.

Inside the Earth

People live on the outer part of the Earth, which is called the crust. This picture shows the Earth with a piece cut out, so that you can see what the inside looks like.

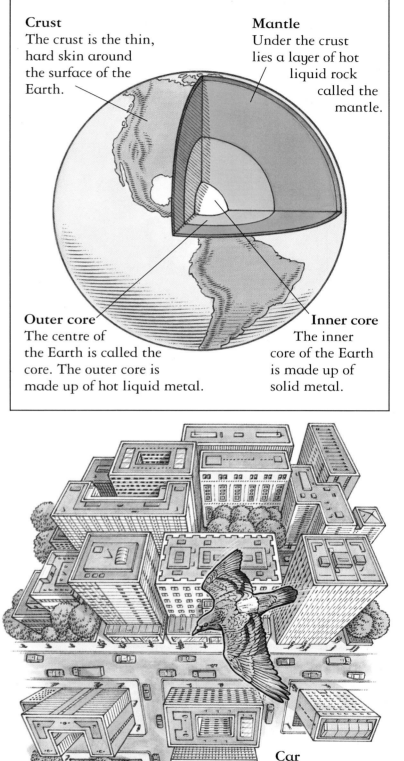

Crust
The crust is the thin, hard skin around the surface of the Earth.

Mantle
Under the crust lies a layer of hot liquid rock called the mantle.

Outer core
The centre of the Earth is called the core. The outer core is made up of hot liquid metal.

Inner core
The inner core of the Earth is made up of solid metal.

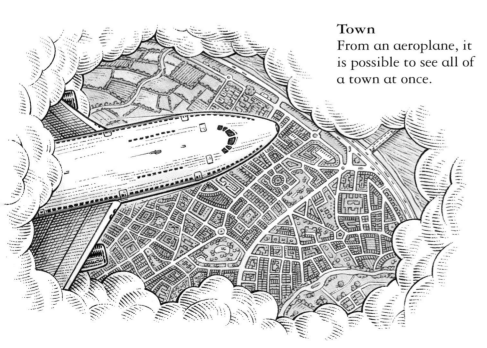

Town
From an aeroplane, it is possible to see all of a town at once.

Car
A car seems smaller, the further away you are from it.

View from a plane

Have you ever looked down from the window of an aeroplane? Some things on the ground are so tiny that you cannot see them. Fields, towns, roads, and rivers look like patterns.

View from a building

Have you ever looked down from the top of a hill or a tall building? From this height, everything looks much smaller. Even large cars look like toys in the streets far below.

What is an atlas?

An atlas is a book of maps or picture information about the world. It shows you the shapes and sizes of parts of the land and sea, and also names them. The maps on these two pages show that land is divided into large areas called continents, while the sea is divided into oceans.

World map
This is a flat map of our round world. The map shows all seven continents at once. Which continent do you live in?

Globe
The Earth spins around an invisible pole, which is called the North Pole at the top, and the South Pole at the bottom. A globe is a round map of the world.

North Pole

Equator

South Pole

The Equator
The Earth is divided by an imaginary line called the Equator, exactly halfway between the North and South Poles. It is hot all year round near the Equator. The further you are from the Equator, the colder it is.

NORTH AMERICA

PACIFIC OCEAN

VENEZUELA
COLOMBIA
GUYANA
SURINAM
FRENCH GUIANA
ECUADOR
PERU
BRAZIL
BOLIVIA
PARAGUAY
ARGENTINA
CHILE
URUGUAY

Compass
Most maps include a North point. If you know where North is, you can find out where you are.

West
West is where the Sun sets in the evening.

North
A compass needle always points to the North Pole.

South
South always lies directly opposite North.

East
East is where the Sun rises in the morning.

Countries
Each continent, except for Australia and Antarctica, is made up of several countries, where people live under different rules and speak different languages.

South America
The continent of South America is made up of 13 different countries.

Map colours
Each country is shown in a different colour to help you read the map.

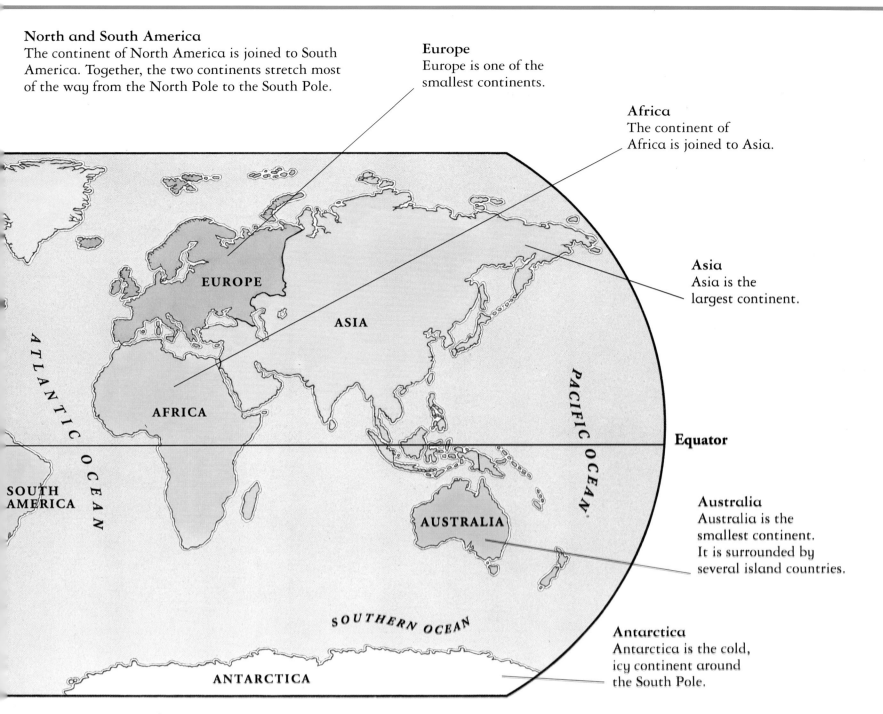

North and South America
The continent of North America is joined to South America. Together, the two continents stretch most of the way from the North Pole to the South Pole.

Europe
Europe is one of the smallest continents.

Africa
The continent of Africa is joined to Asia.

Asia
Asia is the largest continent.

EUROPE

ASIA

ATLANTIC OCEAN

AFRICA

PACIFIC OCEAN

Equator

SOUTH AMERICA

Australia
Australia is the smallest continent. It is surrounded by several island countries.

AUSTRALIA

SOUTHERN OCEAN

Antarctica
Antarctica is the cold, icy continent around the South Pole.

ANTARCTICA

Country borders
Borders mark the line where one country ends and another country begins. Some countries share natural borders, such as a river, lake, or range of mountains.

Natural border
This photo shows the Himalayan mountain range that divides the countries of China and India.

Scale
A world map is a small picture of our enormous world. The countries are shown at the right size, or scale, in relation to each other. The scale on a map helps you to work out how far apart places are.

Flying around the world
If you flew non-stop around the world, it would take you more than two days, flying at a speed of 800 km per hour (800 km/h) or 500 miles per hour (500 mph).

Driving around the world
If you could drive non-stop around the world, it would take you about three weeks, driving at a speed of 80 km/h (50 mph).

World map

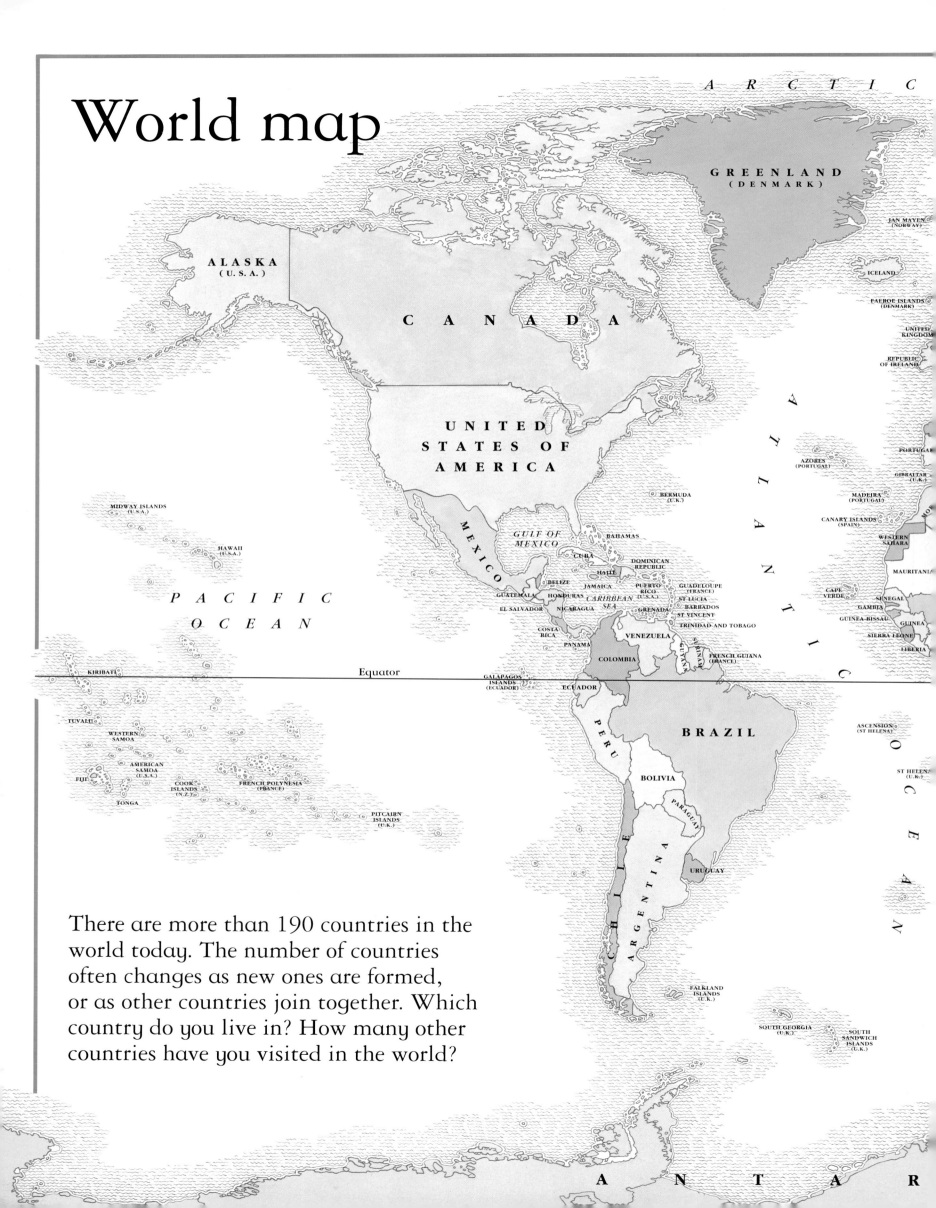

ARCTIC

GREENLAND
(DENMARK)

ALASKA
(U.S.A.)

JAN MAYEN
(NORWAY)

ICELAND

CANADA

FAEROE ISLANDS
(DENMARK)

UNITED
KINGDOM

REPUBLIC
OF IRELAND

UNITED
STATES OF
AMERICA

A
T
L
A
N
T
I
C

PORTUGAL

AZORES
(PORTUGAL)

GIBRALTAR
(U.K.)

MADEIRA
(PORTUGAL)

MIDWAY ISLANDS
(U.S.A.)

BERMUDA
(U.K.)

CANARY ISLANDS
(SPAIN)

WESTERN
SAHARA

HAWAII
(U.S.A.)

GULF OF
MEXICO

BAHAMAS

CUBA

MEXICO

MAURITANIA

PACIFIC
OCEAN

BELIZE
GUATEMALA
EL SALVADOR

HAITI

JAMAICA

HONDURAS
NICARAGUA

DOMINICAN
REPUBLIC

PUERTO
RICO
(U.S.A.)

GUADELOUPE
(FRANCE)

ST LUCIA
BARBADOS
ST VINCENT

CARIBBEAN
SEA

GRENADA

CAPE
VERDE

SENEGAL

GAMBIA

GUINEA-BISSAU

GUINEA

SIERRA LEONE

LIBERIA

COSTA
RICA

PANAMA

VENEZUELA

TRINIDAD AND TOBAGO

GUYANA

SURINAM

FRENCH GUIANA
(FRANCE)

KIRIBATI

Equator

COLOMBIA

GALAPAGOS
ISLANDS
(ECUADOR)

ECUADOR

ASCENSION
(ST HELENA)

TUVALU

WESTERN
SAMOA

PERU

BRAZIL

O
C
E
A
N

ST HELENA
(U.K.)

FIJI

AMERICAN
SAMOA
(U.S.A.)

COOK
ISLANDS
(N.Z.)

FRENCH POLYNESIA
(FRANCE)

BOLIVIA

TONGA

PITCAIRN
ISLANDS
(U.K.)

PARAGUAY

CHILE

ARGENTINA

URUGUAY

There are more than 190 countries in the
world today. The number of countries
often changes as new ones are formed,
or as other countries join together. Which
country do you live in? How many other
countries have you visited in the world?

FALKLAND
ISLANDS
(U.K.)

SOUTH GEORGIA
(U.K.)

SOUTH
SANDWICH
ISLANDS
(U.K.)

ANTAR

SVALBARD
(NORWAY)

NORWAY
SWEDEN
FINLAND
ESTONIA
LATVIA
LITHUANIA
DENMARK
BELORUSSIA
GERMANY
POLAND
TH.
LUX. CZECH REP.
SLOVAKIA
LIECH. AUSTRIA
UKRAINE
CE
SWITZ. HUNG.
SAN MARINO
SLOV.
CROAT.
ROMANIA
MOLDAVIA
CO.
ITALY
BOS. &
HERZE.
YUGO.
BULGARIA
Black Sea
GEORGIA
ANDORRA
VATICAN
CITY
ALB. MACED.
GREECE
TURKEY
ARMENIA
AZERBAIJAN
MALTA
CYPRUS
SYRIA
TUNISIA
MEDITERRANEAN SEA
LEBANON
ISRAEL
IRAQ
JORDAN
KUWAIT
BAHRAIN
QATAR

RUSSIAN FEDERATION

SEA OF
OKHOTSK

KAZAKHSTAN

MONGOLIA

UZBEKISTAN
KYRGYZSTAN
TURKMENISTAN
TAJIKISTAN

CHINA

NORTH
KOREA

SOUTH
KOREA

JAPAN

P A C I F I C
O C E A N

IRAN
AFGHANISTAN
PAKISTAN
NEPAL
BHUTAN

LIBYA
EGYPT
SAUDI
ARABIA
UNITED
ARAB
EMIRATES
OMAN
INDIA
BANGLADESH
BURMA
HONG
KONG
(U.K.)
TAIWAN
MACAO
(PORTUGAL)

PHILIPPINE
SEA

NIGER
CHAD
SUDAN
ERITREA
YEMEN
ARABIAN
SEA
BAY OF
BENGAL
THAILAND
LAOS
VIETNAM
CAMBODIA
SOUTH
CHINA
SEA
PHILIPPINES
GUAM
(U.S.A.)
NORTHERN
MARIANA ISLANDS
(U.S.A.)

NIGERIA
DJIBOUTI
ANDAMAN
ISLANDS
(INDIA)
MARSHALL
ISLANDS
(U.S.A.)

CAMEROON
CENTRAL
AFRICAN
REPUBLIC
ETHIOPIA
SOMALIA
NICOBAR
ISLANDS
(INDIA)
SRI
LANKA
BRUNEI
PALAU
(U.S.A.)
MICRONESIA

ORIAL
UINEA
UGANDA
KENYA
MALDIVES
MALAYSIA
SINGAPORE

GABON
OMB
INCIPE
CONGO
RWANDA
BURUNDI
ZAIRE
TANZANIA
SEYCHELLES
INDONESIA
NAURU

PAPUA
NEW GUINEA
SOLOMON
ISLANDS

ANGOLA
ZAMBIA
COMOROS
I N D I A N

O C E A N
COCOS ISLANDS
(AUSTRALIA)
CHRISTMAS
ISLAND
(AUSTRALIA)
VANUATU

ZIMBABWE
MOZAMBIQUE
MADAGASCAR
MAURITIUS
NEW CALEDONIA
(FRANCE)

NAMIBIA
BOTSWANA
MALAWI
REUNION
(FRANCE)
AUSTRALIA

SWAZILAND

SOUTH
AFRICA
LESOTHO

NEW
ZEALAND

CHATHAM
ISLANDS
(U.K.)

KERGUELEN
(FRANCE)

Capital cities of the world
Every country has a main city, called
its capital. You can find a list of all the
countries of the world that are shown in
this atlas and the names of their capital
cities on pages 44 and 45.

All about maps

Have you ever used a map to help you find your way somewhere? Picture maps show us where things are in a particular place. Usually a map is a flat drawing of an area or a place, called a plan view. There are many different types of maps that help people to travel around in our world.

Mapping a journey

You can find out more about how maps work by drawing one for yourself. The large map on this page shows Peter's journey to school.

Try drawing your own journey to school or to the local shops. To help you, imagine you are a bird looking down on your local area. Think about the things you would pass on your journey and then draw them on your map.

Journey line

Draw a coloured line on your map from your home to your journey's end. This will show the route that you take. Can you name the things that Peter passes on his way to school?

Map keys

Most maps use symbols of real things to give us information about a place. Each symbol is explained on the map in a list called a key.

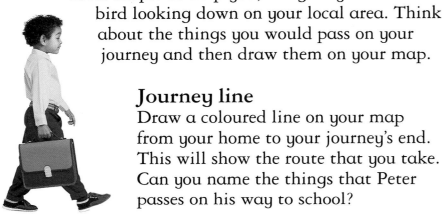

Tree symbol

Peter's picture map uses this tree symbol to show areas where there are lots of trees.

Start of the journey
Start drawing a journey line at the place where your journey begins.

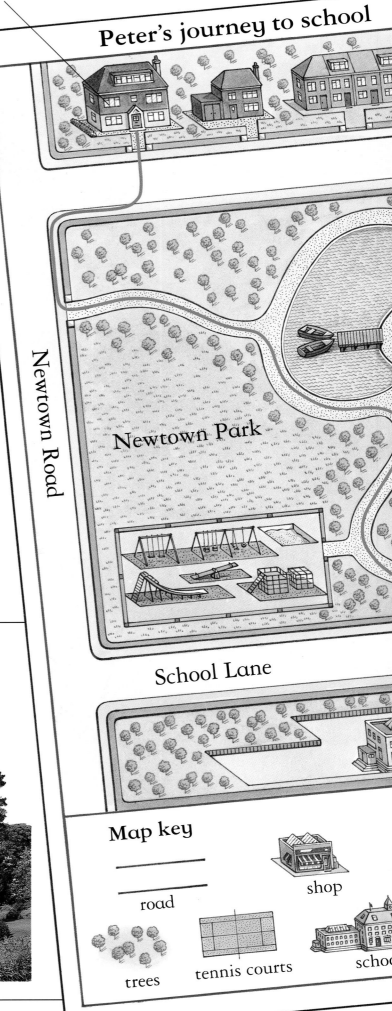

Peter's journey to school

Newtown Road

Newtown Park

School Lane

Map key

_____
road

shop

trees

tennis courts

school

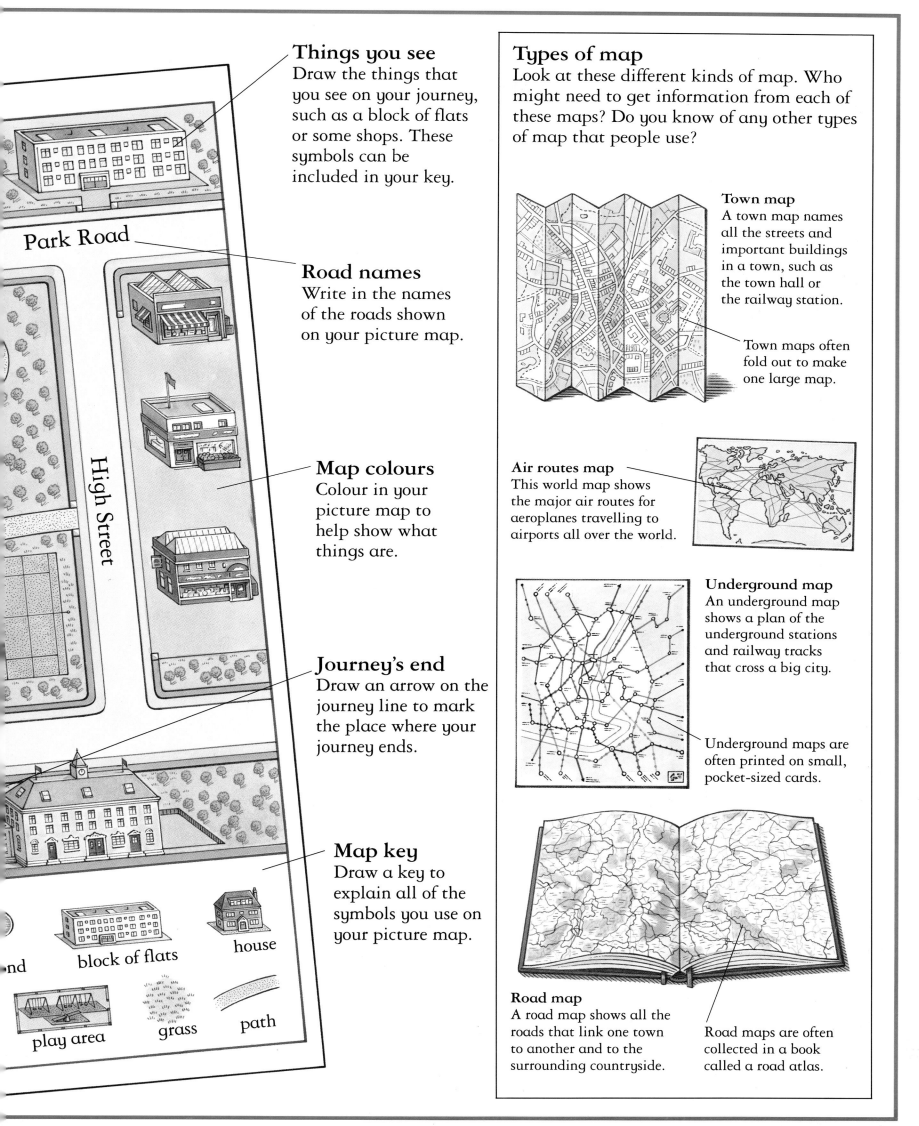

Things you see
Draw the things that you see on your journey, such as a block of flats or some shops. These symbols can be included in your key.

Park Road

High Street

Road names
Write in the names of the roads shown on your picture map.

Map colours
Colour in your picture map to help show what things are.

Journey's end
Draw an arrow on the journey line to mark the place where your journey ends.

Map key
Draw a key to explain all of the symbols you use on your picture map.

block of flats

house

play area

grass

path

Types of map
Look at these different kinds of map. Who might need to get information from each of these maps? Do you know of any other types of map that people use?

Town map
A town map names all the streets and important buildings in a town, such as the town hall or the railway station.

Town maps often fold out to make one large map.

Air routes map
This world map shows the major air routes for aeroplanes travelling to airports all over the world.

Underground map
An underground map shows a plan of the underground stations and railway tracks that cross a big city.

Underground maps are often printed on small, pocket-sized cards.

Road map
A road map shows all the roads that link one town to another and to the surrounding countryside.

Road maps are often collected in a book called a road atlas.

15

Using this atlas

Each map in this book looks at a different region of our world. The picture maps will help you to find out about each continent, its climate and terrain, and the people, plants, and animals that live there.

Map information

This map of West and South Asia is typical of the maps you will find in this book. Read the notes on this page to help you understand the information shown in the pictures on each map.

Locator globe
There is a world globe with every map. The red area on the globe shows where the countries on the map are situated on the Earth.

Natural resources
Drawings on the map show the natural resources, such as oil, that can be found in each region.

Climate and terrain

The climate, or usual weather, in each part of the world affects what the terrain (land) looks like and the people, animals, and plants that live there. The key below explains the types of climate and terrain shown in the maps in this book.

Compass
The compass needle on each map always points to the North Pole, so that you can see in which direction North, South, East, and West are.

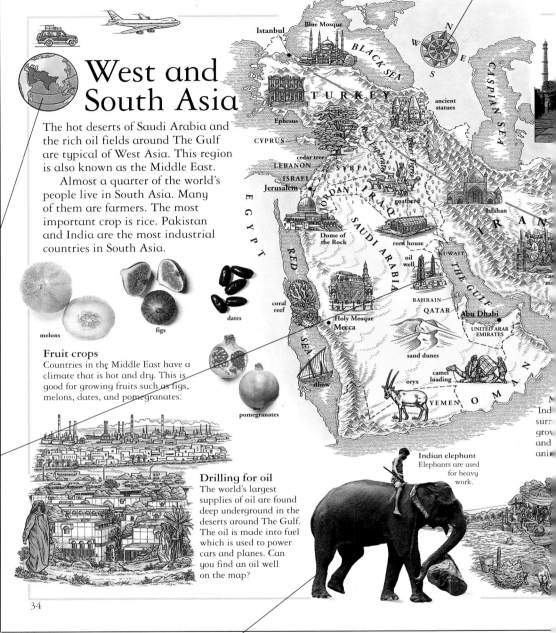

West and South Asia

The hot deserts of Saudi Arabia and the rich oil fields around The Gulf are typical of West Asia. This region is also known as the Middle East.

Almost a quarter of the world's people live in South Asia. Many of them are farmers. The most important crop is rice. Pakistan and India are the most industrial countries in South Asia.

Fruit crops
Countries in the Middle East have a climate that is hot and dry. This is good for growing fruits such as figs, melons, dates, and pomegranates.

melons · figs · dates · pomegranates

Drilling for oil
The world's largest supplies of oil are found deep underground in the deserts around The Gulf. The oil is made into fuel which is used to power cars and planes. Can you find an oil well on the map?

Indian elephant
Elephants are used for heavy work.

34

Colourful photographs
Clear colour photographs show you details of the people, buildings, plants, and animals that are special to each region.

Grassland

Grasslands are flat regions where grass and low bushes grow. Grasslands are home to many different animals.

Rainforest
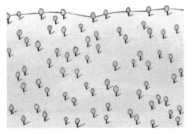
Rainforests are hot, steamy forests that grow in very warm regions near the Equator, where it rains a lot.

Coniferous forest

Forests of conifer trees often grow in cold areas. These evergreen trees keep their leaves all year round.

Deciduous forest
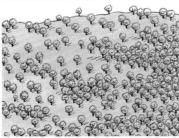
Forests of deciduous trees grow in warmer places. Many deciduous trees lose their leaves in the autumn.

Journey box

The journey box follows the red journey line on each map from one city to another. It tells you how long the journey takes. If you compare the times of different journeys, you will know which continents are larger than others.

Bordering countries
Areas shown in pale yellow are not part of the map. You can find out about these countries on another page.

Animals and plants
Drawings on the map show the animals and plants that live wild in each region.

Buildings
Drawings on the map show typical homes and famous buildings in each region.

Things people do
Drawings on the map show you how people spend their time in each region.

Crops and farming
Drawings on the map show what crops and animals people farm in each region.

Where next?
The signpost at the end of each map tells you in which country you will start the journey on the next page.

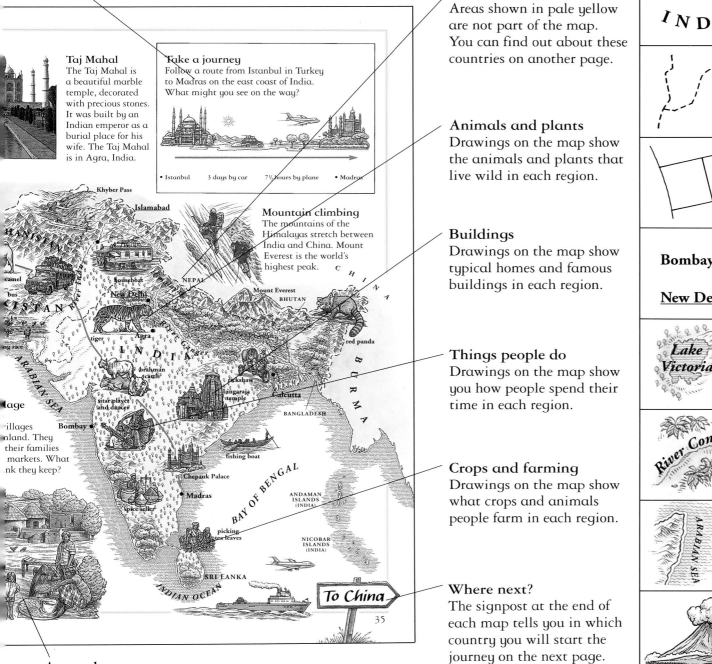

Taj Mahal
The Taj Mahal is a beautiful marble temple, decorated with precious stones. It was built by an Indian emperor as a burial place for his wife. The Taj Mahal is in Agra, India.

Take a journey
Follow a route from Istanbul in Turkey to Madras on the east coast of India. What might you see on the way?

• Istanbul   3 days by car   7½ hours by plane   • Madras

Mountain climbing
The mountains of the Himalayas stretch between India and China. Mount Everest is the world's highest peak.

Artwork scenes
Detailed scenes of people and places show you more about how people live and work in one of the areas shown on the map.

Snow and ice

Some lands are frozen with ice and snow all year long. If the ice melts in summer, then moss and lichen can grow.

Desert

Deserts are very hot or cold areas with little fresh water. Few animals or plants can survive here.

Mountains
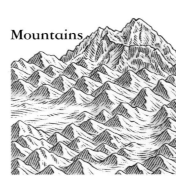
Mountains are high areas of rocky land. Their peaks are often very cold and may be covered with snow.

To China

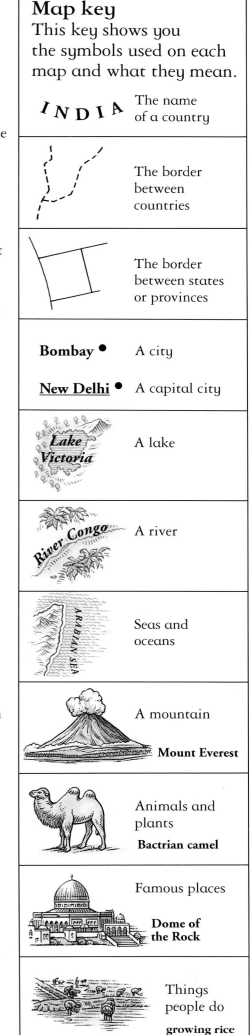

Map key
This key shows you the symbols used on each map and what they mean.

I N D I A	The name of a country
(dashed line)	The border between countries
(line grid)	The border between states or provinces
Bombay ●	A city
New Delhi ●	A capital city
Lake Victoria	A lake
River Congo	A river
ARABIAN SEA	Seas and oceans
(volcano) **Mount Everest**	A mountain
(camel) **Bactrian camel**	Animals and plants
(Dome) **Dome of the Rock**	Famous places
(rice field) **growing rice**	Things people do

Antarctica

Antarctica is the coldest continent on Earth. This land of thick ice and snow surrounds the South Pole. The only creatures that can survive on the icy land are tiny insects. During the summer months, the ice around the edges melts. Penguins and other animals live in the sea and nest on nearby islands.

Take a journey
Follow a journey from Halley Station to Dumont d'Urville Station. There would be nothing to see but ice and snow.

| • Halley Station | 2 days by car | 5 hours by plane | • Dumont d'Urville Station |

Research station
The only people who live in Antarctica are scientists. They live in research stations and travel on sledges with motors, called snowmobiles. Can you find a station on the map?

cruise ship

ATLANTIC OCEAN

leopard seal

South Polar skua

Antarctic cod

Halley Station

snow petrels

emperor penguins

A N T A R C T I C A

Amundsen-Scott Station

SOUTH POLE

elephant seal

Vostok •

krill

ROSS ICE SHELF

Transantarctic Mountains

PACIFIC OCEAN

chinstrap penguins

blue whale

INDIAN OCEAN

Dumont d'Urville Station

humpback whale

Dressed for the cold
Scientists wear special clothes to keep their bodies warm in the freezing cold weather. They come to study the wildlife and learn about the rocks and the weather in this frozen area.

To the Arctic

The Arctic

The most northern part of the Earth is the North Pole. The frozen sea and islands that surround it are called the Arctic. It is so cold here that the Arctic Ocean is frozen for most of the year. Unlike Antarctica, there are many kinds of animals and plants that live here.

grey whales

RUSSIAN FEDERATION

long-tailed skua

walrus

A R C T I C   O C E A N

elk

dog team and snowmobiles

snow goose

CANADA

DEVON ISLAND

ELLESMERE ISLAND

NORTH POLE

hooded seal

musk ox

GREENLAND (DENMARK)

SVALBARD (NORWAY)

killer whale

ptarmigan

lemmings

cod

Polar bear
The polar bear has a thick coat of white fur to keep it warm.

Nuuk

fishing boat

narwhal

Greenland
Greenland is the world's largest island. The town of Nuuk is the country's capital. Here the main industry is fishing for cod and shrimp.

Take a journey
Follow a journey across the Arctic from the North Pole to Nuuk in Greenland. How many different animals might you see on the journey?

| • North Pole | 2 days by car | 5 hours by plane | • Nuuk |

Icebergs
Huge blocks of ice that break away from the frozen sea are called icebergs. These are a danger to ships because only a small part of an iceberg shows above the water. Most of it is hidden under the sea.

To Canada

Canada and Alaska

Canada and Alaska cover the northern half of North America. Canada is the second largest country in the world. However, not many people live there. This is because much of the north of Canada is covered in forests and lakes and is frozen for most of the year. Alaska, which lies to the northwest of Canada, is the largest state in the United States of America. Great supplies of oil have been found there.

Cutting down trees
Many of the pine trees that grow in Canada are cut down and sawn into logs. The logs of wood, called timber, are used to build houses and to make furniture.

Icebreaker ship
This powerful ship is used to break up the thick blocks of ice that form in the cold Arctic Ocean. Can you find the Arctic Ocean on the map?

Growing wheat
In Canada, wheat is grown on vast areas of flat land called the prairies. Wheat is used to make flour for baking into bread. Can you see any wheat fields on the map?

Combine harvester
This giant machine is used to cut and collect the wheat.

polar bear

Arctic hare

BANKS ISLAND

musk ox

VICTO ISLAN

BERING SEA

Arctic fox

ALASKA (U.S.A.)

Yukon River

grizzly bear

Yellowkn

Mount McKinley

YUKON TERRITORY

Mackenzie River

timber

walruses

Rocky Mountains

A

oil tanker

salmon

moose

BRITISH COLUMBIA

ALBER

Fraser River

PACIFIC OCEAN

Vancouver

A R C T I

C

UNITED

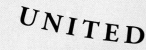

The first Canadians
The first people to live in northern Canada were the Inuit. This Inuit village is on Baffin Island.

Take a journey
The country of Canada is divided into 10 provinces and two northern territories. Follow a route from Vancouver to Ottawa. How many provinces would you pass through on the way?

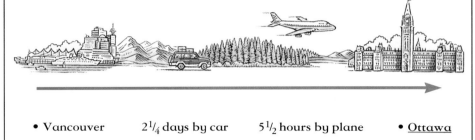

- Vancouver   2¼ days by car   5½ hours by plane   • Ottawa

O C E A N

ELLESMERE ISLAND

G R E E N L A N D
(D E N M A R K)

Baffin Bay

UEEN ZABETH LANDS

ringed seal

BAFFIN ISLAND

Inuit hunters

hooded seal

NORTHWEST TERRITORIES

caribou

Whale watching
People go to watch humpback whales playing in the sea around the coast of Newfoundland. In the cold winter months, they swim south to where the sea is warmer. What other animals live around the coasts of Canada?

N E W F O U N D L A N D

Canada goose

beluga whales

black bear

gannet

PRINCE EDWARD ISLAND

porpoises

N

Hudson Bay

QUEBEC

NEW BRUNSWICK

NOVA SCOTIA

A

ATLANTIC OCEAN

D

MANITOBA

e hockey

KATCHEWAN

beaver

maple trees

Parliament buildings

Lake Winnipeg

O N T A R I O

• Winnipeg

• Ottawa

wheat fields

Lake Superior

Lake Michigan

Lake Ontario

Toronto •

Lake Huron

Niagara Falls

Lake Erie

TES OF AMERICA

To the U.S.A.

United States of America

The United States of America (U.S.A.) is one of the largest countries in the world. It has deserts, mountains, forests, and a vast area of flat land called the Great Plains. Part of North America, the country is made up of 50 states, each with its own capital city. The state of Alaska, shown on page 20, lies to the northwest of Canada.

San Francisco
The city of San Francisco is on the west coast of the U.S.A. The city is built on several hills and people ride on cable-cars that climb the steep streets. Some buildings are designed to survive the earthquakes that happen here.

Grand Canyon
The Grand Canyon is a deep river valley in Arizona. The canyon was formed by the Colorado River cutting through the Rocky Mountains. Can you find the Grand Canyon on the map?

Hawaii
The 50th state of the U.S.A. is a group of islands in the Pacific called Hawaii. Visitors come to surf in the Pacific Ocean and to see the volcanoes.

KAUAI
MOLOKAI
OAHU
MAUI
HAWAII
surfer
Kilauea volcano

CANADA

harvesting wheat

WASHINGTON

salmon

OREGON

skiing

MONTANA

IDAHO

Devils Tower

WYOMIN

cougar

coyote

Rocky Mountains

CALIFORNIA

NEVADA

UNITED STATES

Golden Gate Bridge
San Francisco

UTAH

COLORAD

Colorado River

Grand Canyon

Hollywood

HOLLYWOOD

Los Angeles

ARIZONA

Phoenix

growing oranges

cactus

Pueblo farme

NEW
MEXIC

PACIFIC OCEAN

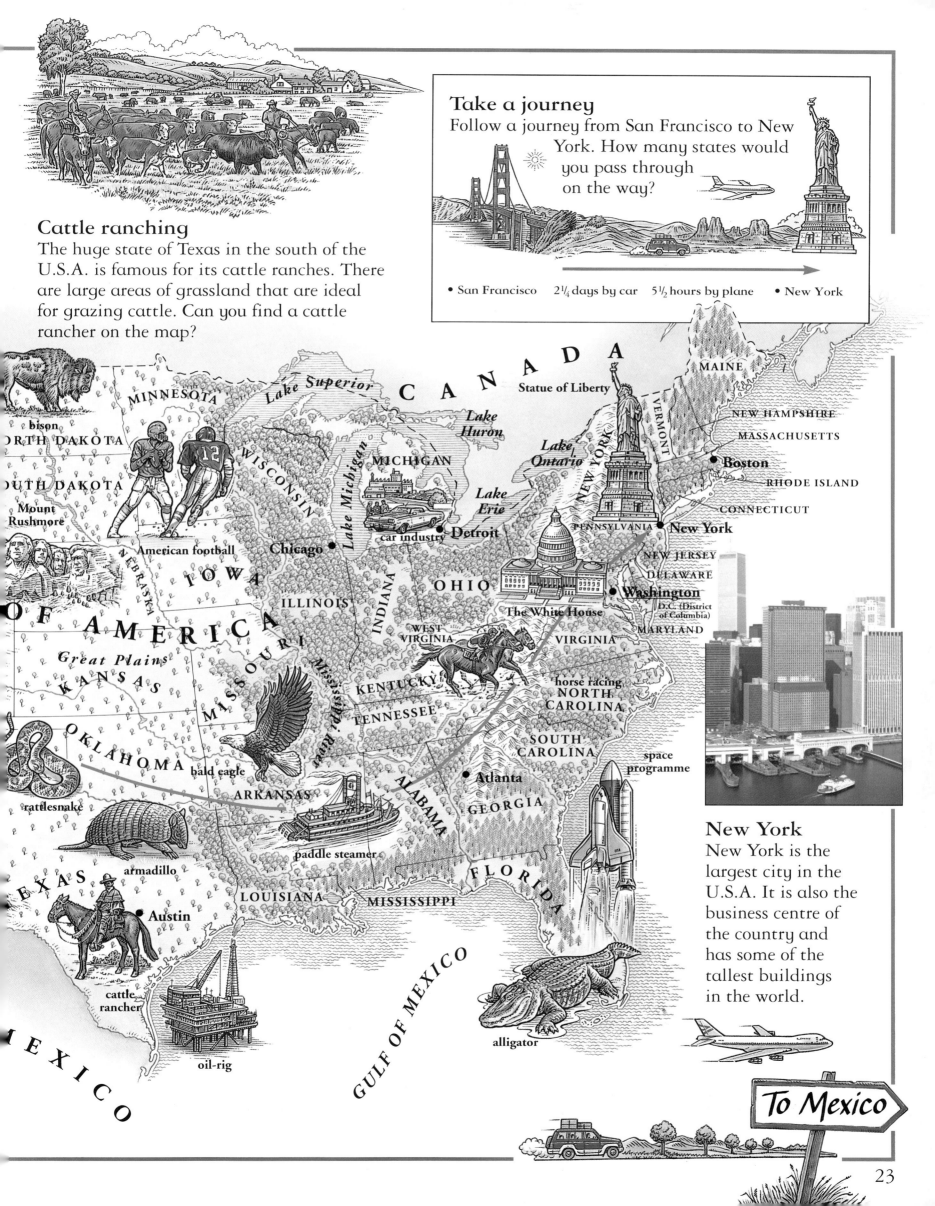

Cattle ranching

The huge state of Texas in the south of the U.S.A. is famous for its cattle ranches. There are large areas of grassland that are ideal for grazing cattle. Can you find a cattle rancher on the map?

Take a journey

Follow a journey from San Francisco to New York. How many states would you pass through on the way?

• San Francisco   2¼ days by car   5½ hours by plane   • New York

CANADA

MAINE

MINNESOTA

Lake Superior

bison

NORTH DAKOTA

WISCONSIN

Lake Huron

MICHIGAN

Lake Ontario

Statue of Liberty

NEW HAMPSHIRE

MASSACHUSETTS

SOUTH DAKOTA

Mount Rushmore

American football

Chicago

Lake Michigan

car industry

Lake Erie

Detroit

NEW YORK

VERMONT

• Boston

RHODE ISLAND

CONNECTICUT

OF AMERICA

NEBRASKA

IOWA

ILLINOIS

INDIANA

OHIO

PENNSYLVANIA

• New York

NEW JERSEY

DELAWARE

Great Plains

The White House

Washington

D.C. (District of Columbia)

MARYLAND

KANSAS

MISSOURI

WEST VIRGINIA

VIRGINIA

KENTUCKY

horse racing

NORTH CAROLINA

Mississippi River

TENNESSEE

OKLAHOMA

bald eagle

rattlesnake

ARKANSAS

SOUTH CAROLINA

space programme

• Atlanta

ALABAMA

GEORGIA

armadillo

paddle steamer

FLORIDA

TEXAS

• Austin

LOUISIANA

MISSISSIPPI

cattle rancher

oil-rig

GULF OF MEXICO

alligator

MEXICO

New York

New York is the largest city in the U.S.A. It is also the business centre of the country and has some of the tallest buildings in the world.

To Mexico

23

Central and South America

Central America is a narrow strip of land that joins North America and South America. The country of Panama has a canal that allows ships to sail from the Atlantic to the Pacific Ocean. Much of South America is rainforest, mountains, or grasslands called pampas. Farmers make money by growing bananas, sugar cane, and coffee. The world's longest chain of mountains, called the Andes, runs down the west coast of South America.

West Indies

In the Caribbean Sea, there are hundreds of large and small islands. These are the West Indies. The sea is usually calm, but the islands sometimes have storms known as hurricanes.

BAHAMAS

coconut trees

CUBA

CAYMAN ISLANDS (U.K.)

JAMAICA

HAITI

DOMINICAN REPUBLIC

PUERTO RICO (U.S.A.)

GUADELOUPE (FRANCE)

ST LUCIA

BARBADOS

GRENADA

TRINIDAD AND TOBAGO

cruise ship

CARIBBEAN SEA

coral reef

Grenada has beautiful beaches.

Buenos Aires

The capital of Argentina is Buenos Aires. It is one of the largest cities in South America and a major port. What products do you think are shipped from here?

Football

Football is a favourite sport in South America. It is played everywhere, even on beaches and in the streets of towns.

Angel Falls

Chichén Itzá

green turtle

Panama Canal

toucan

BELIZE

HONDURAS

GUATEMALA

EL-SALVADOR

NICARAGUA

COSTA RICA

PACIFIC OCEAN

UNITED STATES OF AMERICA

prickly pear

Gila monster

MEXICO

Mexico City

growing avocados

GULF OF MEXICO

N E S W

ATLANTIC OCEAN

FRENCH GUIANA (FRANCE)

capybara

B R A Z I L

growing bananas

cutting sugar cane

Brazil nuts

growing cocoa

Rio de Janeiro

picking coffee

Amazonian Indian

River Amazon

jaguar

market scene

condor

Machu Picchu

P E R U

Andes Mountains

BOLIVIA

ATACAMA DESERT

reed boat

C H I L E

Llamas
Llamas are used to carry goods along narrow mountain roads.

PARAGUAY

gaucho cattle herder

anteater

URUGUAY

Buenos Aires

A R G E N T I N A

Andes Mountains

sheep

fur seals

penguins

FALKLAND ISLANDS (U.K.)

Tierra del Fuego

ATLANTIC OCEAN

The Amazon rainforest
The River Amazon flows through a huge rainforest. Rainforests grow in countries that are hot and have a lot of rain. Many kinds of birds, animals, and plants live there.

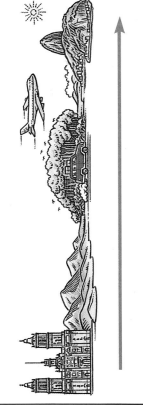

To the U.K.

Ancient city
The ruins of a very old city can be seen in Machu Picchu, Peru. These ruins tell us about the Incas, the people who lived there hundreds of years ago. Can you find Machu Picchu on the map?

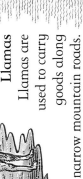

The people of Peru
Many of the people of Peru live in villages in the mountains of the Andes. The farmers grow maize, potatoes, and beans. The women use animal hair to weave colourful cloth, which they sell in local markets.

Take a journey
Follow a journey from Mexico City in Mexico to Rio de Janeiro in Brazil. How many countries would you pass through on the way?

• Mexico City   4 days by car   10 hours by plane   • Rio de Janeiro

North Europe

The countries of Denmark, Norway, and Sweden make up the area called Scandinavia. Finland also borders the Baltic Sea and Iceland lies in the Atlantic Ocean. Much of the land has lakes, forests, and mountains and is covered with snow during the winter months. The United Kingdom (U.K.) is made up of England, Northern Ireland, Scotland, and Wales. Europe has many important natural resources, such as oil and gas from the North Sea, timber from the forests, and fish in the surrounding seas.

Iceland

Iceland is often called the land of ice and fire. This cold and windy island is covered with huge sheets of ice and there are also many volcanoes. Fountains of hot water, called geysers, are forced out of the ground.

London

London is the capital city of the United Kingdom. The British government makes laws in the Houses of Parliament. These buildings form the Palace of Westminster, which has a famous clock tower known as Big Ben.

Big Ben

Take a journey

Follow a route from Plymouth in England to Edinburgh in Scotland. What might you see on the way?

• Plymouth   10 hours by car   1 hour by plane   • Edinburgh

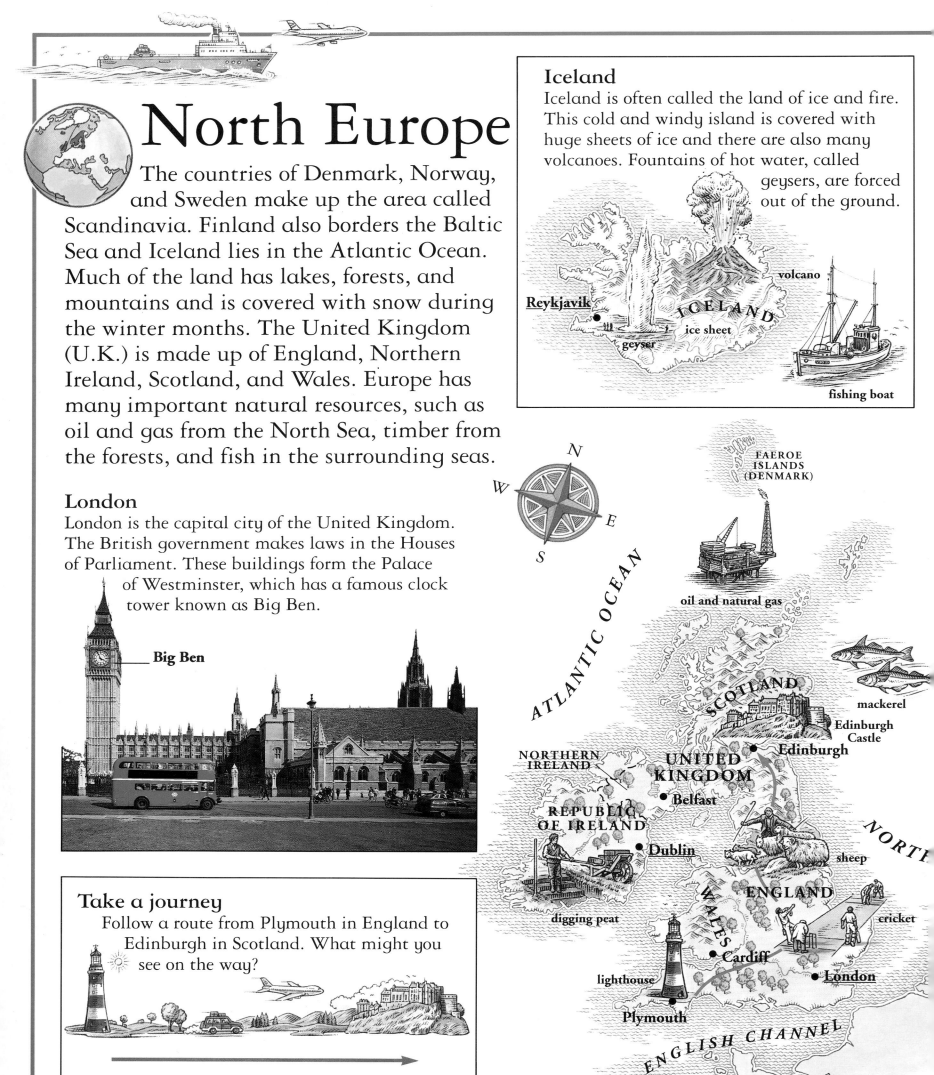

Reykjavik

volcano

ICELAND

ice sheet

geyser

fishing boat

N
W
S
E

FAEROE ISLANDS (DENMARK)

ATLANTIC OCEAN

oil and natural gas

mackerel

SCOTLAND

Edinburgh Castle

Edinburgh

NORTHERN IRELAND

UNITED KINGDOM

Belfast

REPUBLIC OF IRELAND

Dublin

sheep

NORTH

digging peat

ENGLAND

WALES

cricket

Cardiff

lighthouse

London

Plymouth

ENGLISH CHANNEL

FRANCE

Coast of Norway

The coast of Norway has lots of inlets with steep sides. These are called fjords. They were made thousands of years ago by ice cutting into the land.

eagle

lynx

Sami family

wolf

Reindeer

The reindeer is a kind of large deer that lives in cold regions. The Sami people keep large herds of reindeer and use their fur to make clothes. Can you find the Sami people on the map?

ARCTIC OCEAN

Tromso

SWEDEN

NORWAY

FINLAND

GULF OF BOTHNIA

hydroelectric power

paper mill

seals

Bergen

Oslo

Helsinki

Tallinn

saw mill

stave church

Lake Vanern

Stockholm

ESTONIA

BALTIC SEA

glass blower

Riga

LATVIA

houses in Riga

SKAGERRAK

KATTEGAT

pig farming

LITHUANIA

DENMARK

Copenhagen

fishing boat

Vilnius

EA

POLAND

Timber industry

Pine and fir trees grow in the cold forests of Sweden, Norway, and Finland. They provide wood, which is used to make paper for books and newspapers.

Pine cones
Pine trees grow their seeds in hard, wooden cones.

Take a journey

Follow a route from Tromso in Norway to Riga in Latvia. How many countries would you pass through on your journey?

| • Tromso | 1 day by car | 2¼ hours by plane | • Riga |

To the Netherlands

Central Europe

Many of the countries in Central Europe are fairly flat. Most of the main cities and industries are in the north. Further east, in Poland and Hungary, the land is used for farming and coal-mining. Several long rivers run through Europe. They are used to transport goods from one place to another. In the south, there are high, snow-capped mountains called the Alps. The Alps stretch from France through Italy, Switzerland, and Austria.

NORTH SEA

canal boat

Amsterdam

NETHERLANDS

making sausages

storks

Berlin

Brandenburg Gate

Brussels

making chocolates

BELGIUM

River Rhine

making cars

Frankfurt

red deer

Luxembourg

LUXEMBOURG

GERMANY

N
W · E
S

Munich

Neuschwanstein Castle

FRANCE

SWITZERLAND

Berne

Alps

AUSTRIA

LIECHTENSTEIN

ITALY

Matterhorn

The Alps

The scenery in the Alps is very pretty. There are forests, lakes, and rivers. Many people visit the mountains for skiing holidays. Special lifts take them up to the snow. Can you find any other mountains on the map?

Alpine flowers

High up in the mountains, small flowers grow between the rocks or low on the ground. This keeps them out of the cold winds.

Blue gentian

St. John's ragwort

Ship-building

Ship-building is an important industry in Poland. Ships are made from steel. Coal and iron are mined in Poland and used to make the steel. There are ports for ships on the coast of the Baltic Sea. Can you find the port of Gdansk on the map?

Windmill

A windmill is powered by the wind, which turns four large sails. Can you find a windmill on the map?

Dutch tulips

The flat fields in the Netherlands are used for farming. Many Dutch farmers grow flowers, such as tulips. Windmills pump water into the fields.

Take a journey

Follow a route from Amsterdam in the Netherlands to Budapest in Hungary. What might you see in the different countries on the way?

| • Amsterdam | 20 hours by car | 2 hours by plane | • Budapest |

Map labels:

BALTIC SEA

RUSSIAN FEDERATION

LITHUANIA

BELORUSSIA

Gdansk

wooden windmill

European bison

POLAND

River Oder

coal-mining

Warsaw

River Vistula

growing sugar beet

sheep

UKRAINE

River Elbe

Prague

CZECH REPUBLIC

Cathedral of St Vitus

Carpathian Mountains

SLOVAKIA

Vienna

Bratislava

River Danube

Budapest

Parliament building

ROMANIA

Alps

Lipizzaner horse

HUNGARY

street market

SLOVENIA

CROATIA

YUGOSLAVIA

To Portugal

South Europe

The southern countries of Europe have many historical cities with famous buildings to visit. They also have important industries such as steelworks and car-making. These countries have hot, dry summers. The weather is good for growing oranges, tomatoes, and olives. Grapes are grown in many countries, such as France, and are used to make wine.

Along the coast

Most countries in South Europe have a coastline. Many people in Spain and Portugal make their living by fishing. Tourists also come to enjoy the sunny beaches. Can you find any tourists on the Greek island of Crete?

Water sports

In the warm Mediterranean Sea, water sports such as windsurfing and sailing are very popular. People like to sail along the coast and around the islands.

Map labels:
UNITED KINGDOM
ENGLISH CHANNEL
Eiffel Tower
Paris
FRANCE
BAY OF BISCAY
vineyard
pig farming
brown bear
Camargue horses
Bilbao
River Ebro
ANDORRA
PORTUGAL
Royal Palace
Barcelona
Belem Tower
Madrid
SPAIN
yacht
MENOR
Lisbon
flamenco dancers
Valencia
MALLORCA
Seville
picking oranges
IBIZA
MEDITERRANEA
lobster

Take a journey

Follow a route across Europe, from Lisbon in Portugal to Athens in Greece. How many countries would you pass through on the way?

• Lisbon   2¼ days by car   5½ hours by plane   • Athens

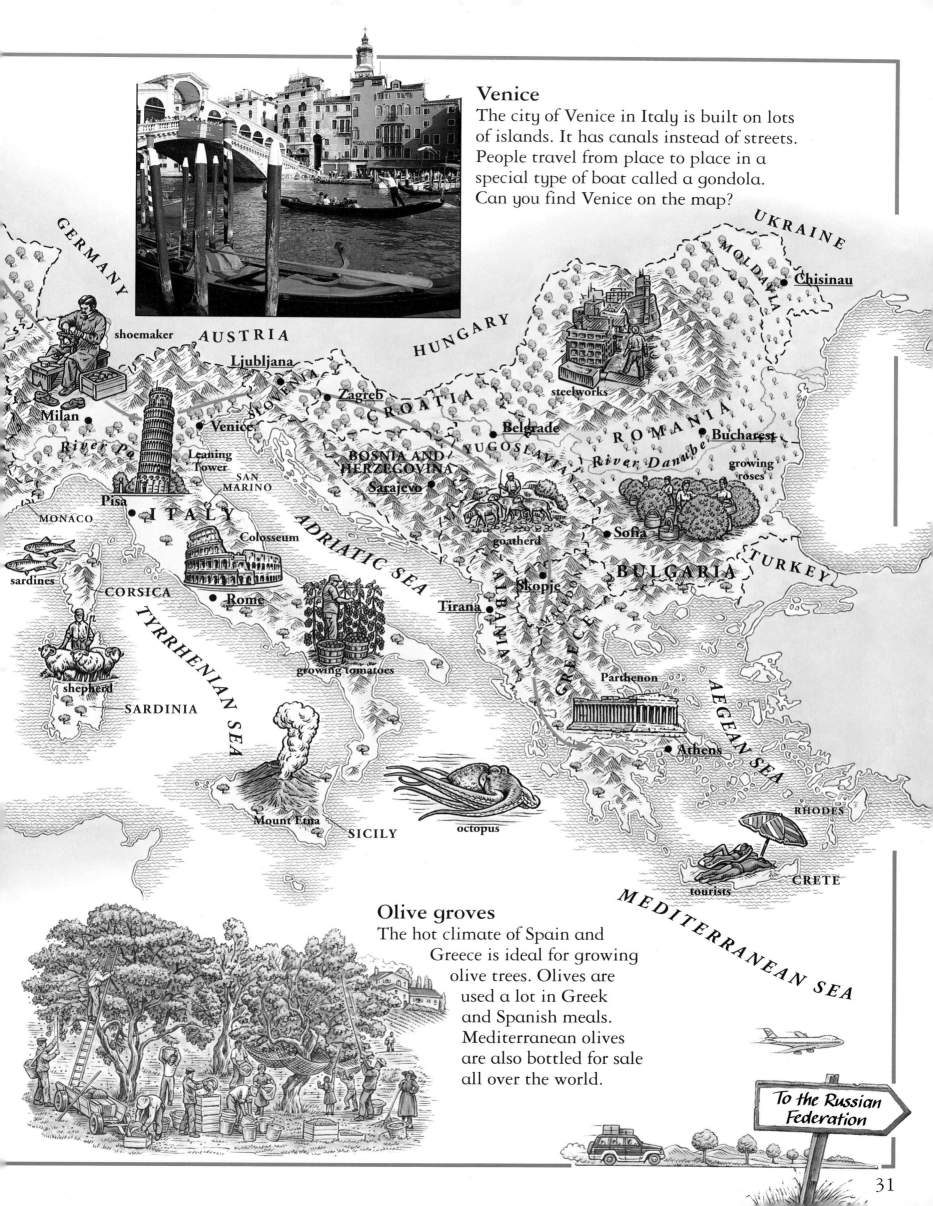

Venice

The city of Venice in Italy is built on lots of islands. It has canals instead of streets. People travel from place to place in a special type of boat called a gondola. Can you find Venice on the map?

UKRAINE

MOLDAVIA

Chisinau

GERMANY

shoemaker

AUSTRIA

HUNGARY

steelworks

ROMANIA

Ljubljana

SLOVENIA

Zagreb

CROATIA

Belgrade

YUGOSLAVIA

Bucharest

River Danube

Milan

Venice

River Po

Leaning Tower

SAN MARINO

BOSNIA AND HERZEGOVINA

Sarajevo

growing roses

Pisa

ITALY

Colosseum

MONACO

goatherd

Sofia

sardines

CORSICA

Rome

BULGARIA

TURKEY

ADRIATIC SEA

Skopje

Tirana

ALBANIA

GREECE

TYRRHENIAN SEA

shepherd

SARDINIA

growing tomatoes

Parthenon

AEGEAN SEA

Athens

Mount Etna

SICILY

octopus

RHODES

CRETE

tourists

MEDITERRANEAN SEA

Olive groves

The hot climate of Spain and Greece is ideal for growing olive trees. Olives are used a lot in Greek and Spanish meals. Mediterranean olives are also bottled for sale all over the world.

To the Russian Federation

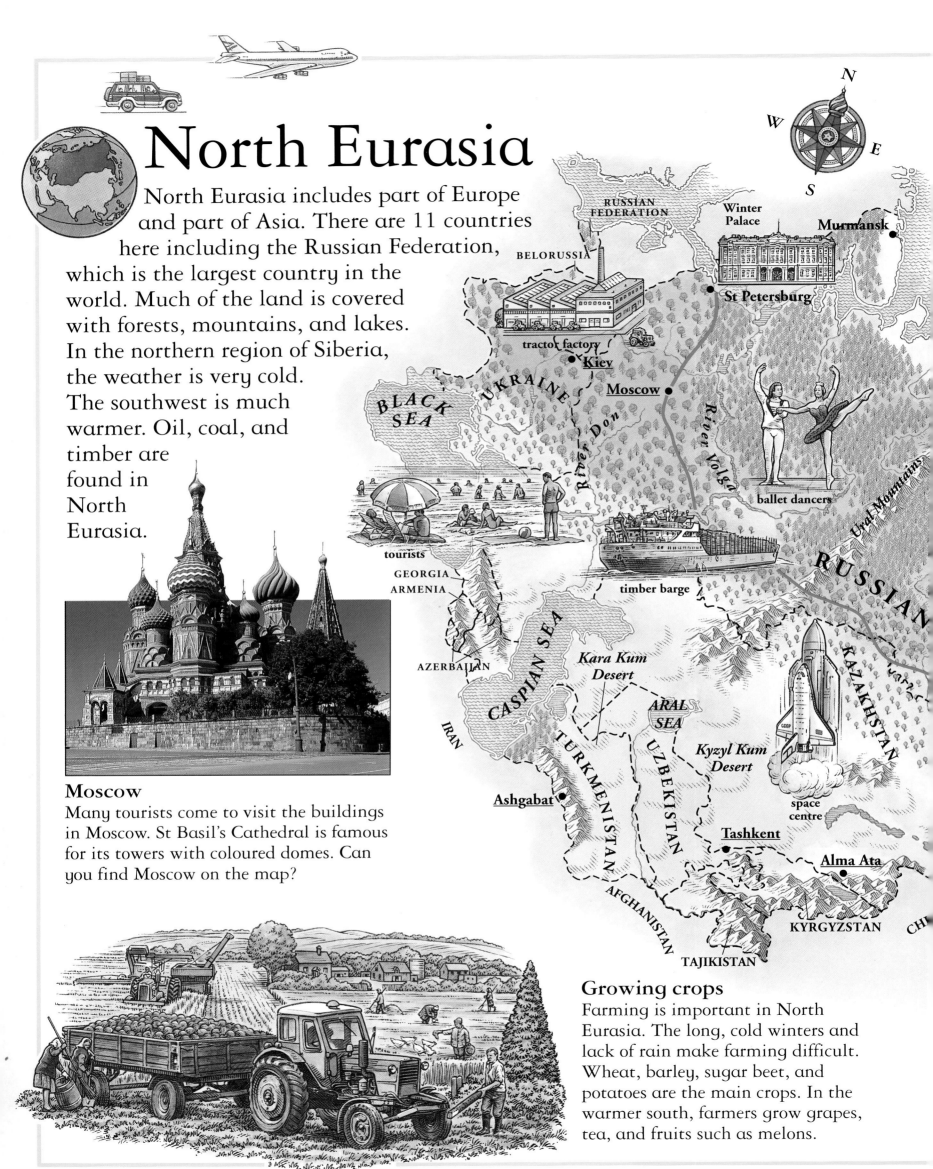

North Eurasia

North Eurasia includes part of Europe and part of Asia. There are 11 countries here including the Russian Federation, which is the largest country in the world. Much of the land is covered with forests, mountains, and lakes. In the northern region of Siberia, the weather is very cold. The southwest is much warmer. Oil, coal, and timber are found in North Eurasia.

Moscow
Many tourists come to visit the buildings in Moscow. St Basil's Cathedral is famous for its towers with coloured domes. Can you find Moscow on the map?

Growing crops
Farming is important in North Eurasia. The long, cold winters and lack of rain make farming difficult. Wheat, barley, sugar beet, and potatoes are the main crops. In the warmer south, farmers grow grapes, tea, and fruits such as melons.

Map labels:
RUSSIAN FEDERATION · BELORUSSIA · Winter Palace · Murmansk · St Petersburg · tractor factory · Kiev · Moscow · River Don · River Volga · ballet dancers · BLACK SEA · UKRAINE · Ural Mountains · RUSSIAN · tourists · timber barge · GEORGIA · ARMENIA · AZERBAIJAN · CASPIAN SEA · IRAN · Kara Kum Desert · ARAL SEA · Kyzyl Kum Desert · KAZAKHSTAN · space centre · TURKMENISTAN · UZBEKISTAN · Ashgabat · Tashkent · Alma Ata · AFGHANISTAN · KYRGYZSTAN · CHI · TAJIKISTAN

N · W · E · S

ice-breaker ship

FRANZ JOSEF LAND

Coal fields
There are large coal fields in the Ukraine, Kazakhstan, and east Siberia. Much of the coal is used to supply power stations or to provide fuel for factories. What types of factory can you find on this map?

BERING STRAIT

NOVAYA ZEMLYA

SEVERNAYA ZEMLYA

ARCTIC OCEAN

grey whales

NEW SIBERIAN ISLANDS

BERING SEA

River Kolyma

reindeer herder

wooden house (dacha)

paper factory

Siberian leopard

oil-rigs

Kamchatka volcano

SIBERIA   *River Lena*

FEDERATION

fishing boat

packing fish

Trans-Siberian Railway

Lake Baikal

Irkutsk

Altai Mountains

MONGOLIA

CHINA

KURILE ISLANDS

Vladivostok

Take a journey
Follow a route across the Russian Federation from St Petersburg to Vladivostok. What might you see on the way?

• St Petersburg   4$\frac{1}{3}$ days by car   10$\frac{1}{2}$ hours by plane   • Vladivostok

To Turkey

West and South Asia

The hot deserts of Saudi Arabia and the rich oil fields around The Gulf are typical of West Asia. This region is also known as the Middle East.

Almost a quarter of the world's people live in South Asia. Many of them are farmers. The most important crop is rice. Pakistan and India are the most industrial countries in South Asia.

melons

figs

dates

Fruit crops
Countries in the Middle East have a climate that is hot and dry. This is good for growing fruits such as figs, melons, dates, and pomegranates.

pomegranates

Drilling for oil
The world's largest supplies of oil are found deep underground in the deserts around The Gulf. The oil is made into fuel which is used to power cars and planes. Can you find an oil well on the map?

Istanbul
Blue Mosque
BLACK SEA
TURKEY
ancient statues
Ephesus
CYPRUS
River Euphrates
River Tigris
cedar tree
LEBANON
SYRIA
ISRAEL
Jerusalem
JORDAN
IRAQ
goatherd
EGYPT
Dome of the Rock
SAUDI ARABIA
reed house
oil well
KUWAIT
RED SEA
coral reef
BAHRAIN
QATAR
Abu Dhal
THE GULF
UNITED EMIRA
Holy Mosque
Mecca
sand dunes
camel loading
oryx
dhow
YEMEN
O

Indian elephant
Elephants are used for heavy work.

Taj Mahal

The Taj Mahal is a beautiful marble temple, decorated with precious stones. It was built by an Indian emperor as a burial place for his wife. The Taj Mahal is in Agra, India.

Take a journey

Follow a route from Istanbul in Turkey to Madras on the east coast of India. What might you see on the way?

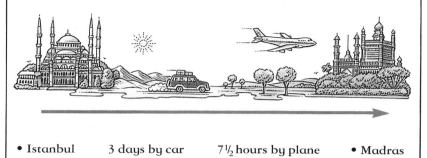

• Istanbul   3 days by car   7½ hours by plane   • Madras

Mountain climbing

The mountains of the Himalayas stretch between India and China. Mount Everest is the world's highest peak.

Indian village

Many people in India still live in villages surrounded by farmland. They grow crops to feed their families and to sell at local markets. What animals do you think they keep?

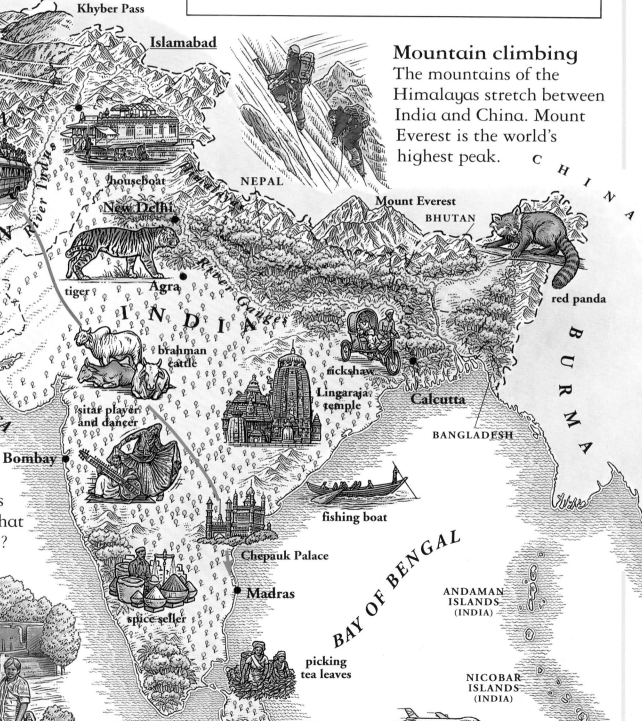

Khyber Pass

Islamabad

AFGHANISTAN

Bactrian camel

carpet making

bus

PAKISTAN

River Indus

houseboat

New Delhi

NEPAL

Mount Everest

BHUTAN

CHINA

red panda

growing rice

tiger

Agra

INDIA

River Ganges

oil tanker

ARABIAN SEA

brahman cattle

rickshaw

Lingaraja temple

Calcutta

BANGLADESH

BURMA

sitar player and dancer

Bombay

fishing boat

Chepauk Palace

Madras

spice seller

BAY OF BENGAL

ANDAMAN ISLANDS (INDIA)

picking tea leaves

NICOBAR ISLANDS (INDIA)

SRI LANKA

INDIAN OCEAN

To China

East Asia

The countries of East Asia cover a large part of the mainland as well as many islands. China is the largest country and has deserts and high mountains in the region of Tibet. Most people live in the east, where the land is good for growing tea, rice, and wheat. Further south, the countries are hotter. Farmers grow crops such as rubber trees, tobacco plants, and pineapples.

mosque

Kashgar

Bactrian camel

Takla Makan Desert

K2 Mountain

Great Wall of China

TIBET

Chongqing

Himalayas

lammergeier

INDIA

terracotta army

BAY OF BENGAL

BURMA

LAOS

THAILAND

CAMBODIA

floating market

SOUTH CHINA SEA

SUMATRA

rubber trees

SINGAPORE

Jakarta

Rice growing

Rice is an important crop in countries such as Thailand and Malaysia. The hot climate and heavy rains during the monsoon are good for growing rice. Farmers use flat land and also cut fields into the steep hillsides. Can you find Thailand on the map?

N W E S

Take a journey

Follow a route from Kashgar in China to Hong Kong. What interesting sights might you see on the way?

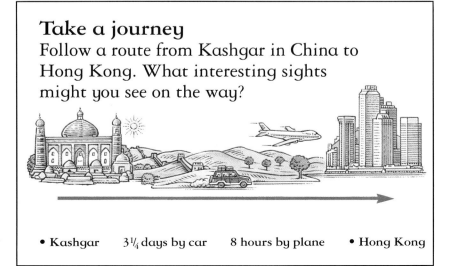

• Kashgar   3¼ days by car   8 hours by plane   • Hong Kong

The streets of China

More people live in China than in any other country. Many people travel around the busy cities by bike.

FEDERATION

fossil hunting

Gobi Desert

low River

tiger

NORTH KOREA

● **Peking (Beijing)**

Seoul ●

SOUTH KOREA

picking tea leaves

River Yangtze

● **Shanghai**

EAST CHINA SEA

JAPAN

TAIWAN

● **Hong Kong** (U.K.)

MACAO (PORTUGAL)

AINAN

oil tanker

SOUTH CHINA SEA

PHILIPPINES

Manila ● **LUZON**

MINDANAO

BRUNEI

SIA

RNEO

orang-utan

CELEBES

MOLUCCAS

DONESIA

BANDA SEA

IRIAN JAYA (INDONESIA)

PAPUA NEW GUINEA

AVA

TIMOR

BALI

AUSTRALIA

Pandas
Giant pandas live in the cool mountains of central China. They feed on the bamboo plants that grow there. What other animals can you find in East Asia?

Japan
Japan is made up of hundreds of islands. The four main islands are Honshu, Hokkaido, Kyushu, and Shikoku. Mountains and woods cover much of the land. Most people live on the coasts or in big cities like Tokyo. On the island of Honshu there is a volcano named Mount Fuji. Can you find it on the map?

cranes

Tokyo
Tokyo is the capital city of Japan. Many people work in factories, which make cars, cameras, and electronic goods. The city also has beautiful gardens where people can walk and relax.

HOKKAIDO

HONSHU

JAPAN

Shinto temple

Mount Fuji

● **Tokyo**

SHIKOKU

loggerhead turtle

KYUSHU

Fishing
Japanese people eat lots of fish. Japan catches more fish than any other country and has the world's biggest fleet of fishing boats.

To Algeria

Africa

Africa is a huge, hot continent. It has the world's largest desert, the Sahara. Most Africans are farmers, and the food that they grow is sent all over the world. People also live and work in the crowded cities. There are many types of terrain in Africa, including deserts, grasslands, and rainforests. Many different birds and animals live here.

Water in the desert
An oasis is a place in the desert where water is found. Can you find an oasis on the map?

Lovebird
The lovebird is one of many birds that live in the rainforest.

Living by the river
In the rainforest, people build houses on stilts along the rivers where they live. Can you find the River Congo on the map?

Underground treasure
South Africa has many gold and diamond mines. Most of the diamonds used to make jewellery are found in South Africa.

gold

diamond

Take a journey
Follow a route across Africa, from Algiers in Algeria to Cape Town in South Africa. What might you see on the way?

• Algiers   4 days by car   10 hours by plane   • Cape Town

Map labels: MOROCCO, Algiers, carpet seller, ALGERIA, TUNISIA, WESTERN SAHARA, camel train, Sahara Desert, nomad camp, MAURITANIA, round hut, market, Tuareg horseman, MALI, NIGER, SENEGAL, GAMBIA, GUINEA-BISSAU, BURKINA, River Niger, Lake Chad, GUINEA, SIERRA LEONE, NIGERIA, LIBERIA, Lagos, IVORY COAST, GHANA, TOGO, BENIN, container ship, ATLANTIC OCEAN, CAMEROON, EQUATORIAL GUINEA, flying fish, GABON, CONGO, hornbill

MEDITERRANEAN SEA

Suez Canal

LIBYA

pyramids

Cairo

EGYPT

River Nile

oasis

ostrich

CHAD

hippopotamus

crocodile

SUDAN

pelican

RED SEA

SAUDI ARABIA

ERITREA

DJIBOUTI

ETHIOPIA

Great Rift Valley

goatherds

CENTRAL AFRICAN REPUBLIC

gorilla

River Congo

ZAIRE

UGANDA

KENYA

SOMALIA

elephant

RWANDA

BURUNDI

Lake Victoria

Mount Kenya

Mombasa

INDIAN OCEAN

ANGOLA

elephants

masked dancer

Kilimanjaro

TANZANIA

MALAWI

giraffe

ZAMBIA

River Zambezi

giraffe

lemur

NAMIBIA

zebra

ZIMBABWE

Victoria Falls

MOZAMBIQUE

MADAGASCAR

BOTSWANA

Ndebele house

chameleon

springbok

SWAZILAND

SOUTH AFRICA

LESOTHO

Cape Town

Animals of the grasslands

Tourists come from all over the world to see the animals that live safely in Africa's nature reserves. Can you name some animals from the grasslands?

Lion
Lions hunt zebras and wildebeest that live in the hot grasslands.

Mombasa

Mombasa is a big, modern city on the coast of Kenya. Many thousands of people work in its factories, offices, and shops. The huge elephant tusks at the entrance to the city are made of metal.

To Australia

Australasia

Australia is the smallest of the seven continents. It is the largest island in the Pacific Ocean, in an area known as Australasia. The first people to live in Australia were the Aboriginals. Although Australia is a big country, it is not very crowded because large areas are hot desert. Most people live in cities near the coast, where it is cooler.

INDONESIA

ARAFURA SEA

Darwin

GULF OF CARPENTARIA

Aboriginal dancers

NORTHERN TERRITORY

red kangaroos

flying doctor

packing fruit

INDIAN OCEAN

frilled lizard

WESTERN AUSTRALIA

Gibson Desert

A U S T R A L I A

Uluru (Ayers Rock)

Simpson Desert

koalas

SOUTH AUSTRALIA

Indian Pacific Railway

Perth

Nullarbor Plain

great white shark

Adelaide

River Darling

River Mur

VICTOR
Melbourne

TASMAN

Hobart

Sheep farming

The central plains of Australia are called the outback. In these dry areas there are huge sheep farms called stations. Farmers shear sheep for wool, which is sold to other countries. What other animals can you see on the map?

Take a journey

Follow a route across Australia from Perth to Sydney. What might you see on the journey?

• Perth   2¼ days by car   5½ hours by plane   • Sydney

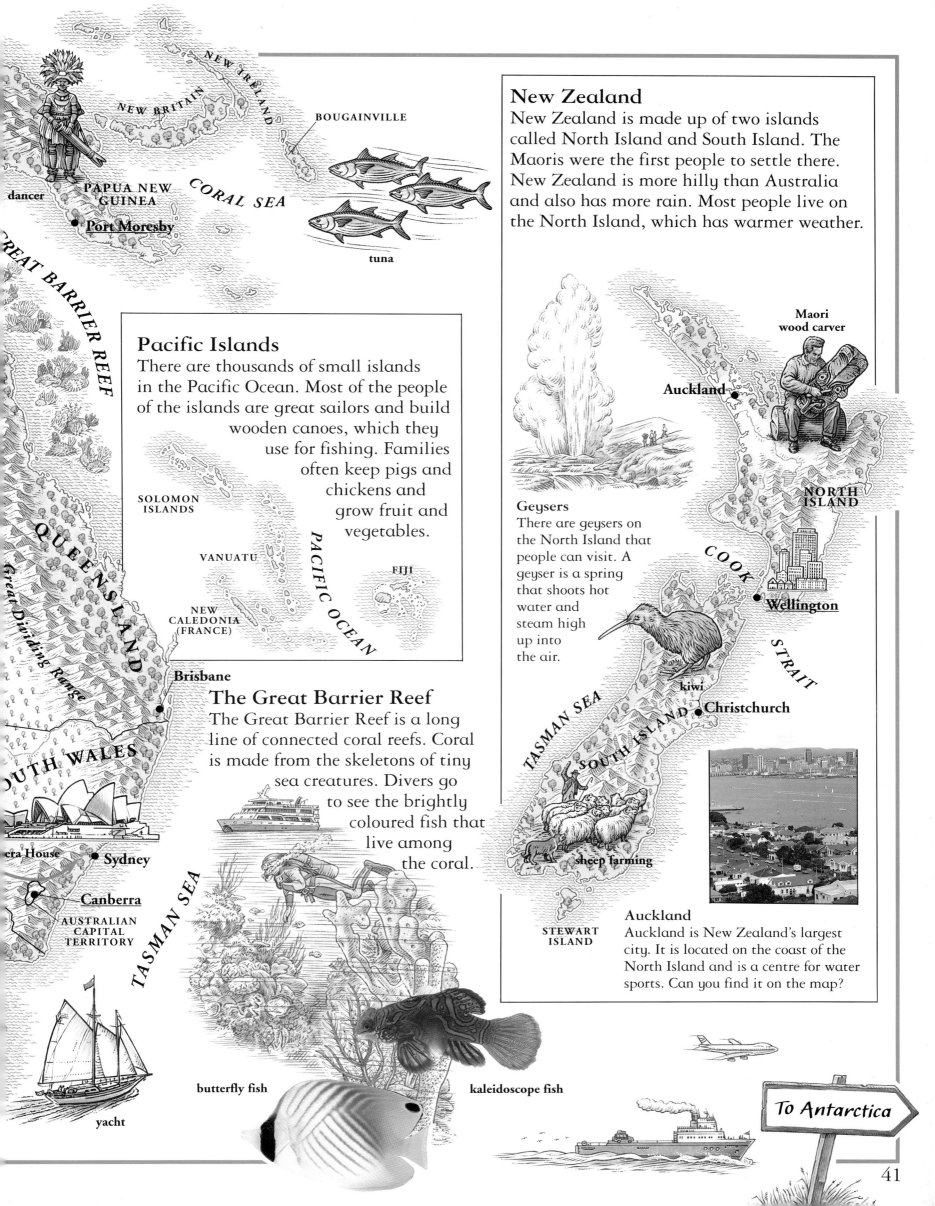

dancer

BOUGAINVILLE

PAPUA NEW GUINEA

CORAL SEA

● **Port Moresby**

tuna

New Zealand

New Zealand is made up of two islands called North Island and South Island. The Maoris were the first people to settle there. New Zealand is more hilly than Australia and also has more rain. Most people live on the North Island, which has warmer weather.

Maori wood carver

Auckland

Pacific Islands

There are thousands of small islands in the Pacific Ocean. Most of the people of the islands are great sailors and build wooden canoes, which they use for fishing. Families often keep pigs and chickens and grow fruit and vegetables.

SOLOMON ISLANDS

VANUATU

FIJI

PACIFIC OCEAN

NEW CALEDONIA (FRANCE)

Geysers
There are geysers on the North Island that people can visit. A geyser is a spring that shoots hot water and steam high up into the air.

NORTH ISLAND

COOK STRAIT

Wellington

kiwi

Brisbane

The Great Barrier Reef

The Great Barrier Reef is a long line of connected coral reefs. Coral is made from the skeletons of tiny sea creatures. Divers go to see the brightly coloured fish that live among the coral.

TASMAN SEA

SOUTH ISLAND

Christchurch

GREAT BARRIER REEF

QUEENSLAND

Great Dividing Range

SOUTH WALES

era House

● **Sydney**

Canberra

AUSTRALIAN CAPITAL TERRITORY

TASMAN SEA

sheep farming

STEWART ISLAND

Auckland
Auckland is New Zealand's largest city. It is located on the coast of the North Island and is a centre for water sports. Can you find it on the map?

yacht

butterfly fish

kaleidoscope fish

To Antarctica

41

Our amazing world

Here are some record-breaking facts and figures about some of the places in our amazing world. Can you find these places in your atlas?

Did you know?

The Earth spins around at 1,600 km/h (1,000 mph).

The largest iceberg ever seen was floating off Antarctica. It was larger than the whole of Belgium.

The longest river is the River Nile in Africa. It is 6,670 km (4,145 miles) long.

The largest forest covers part of the Russian Federation and Finland. It is larger than the whole of the U.S.A.

The largest ocean is the Pacific. It is larger than all of the land in the world put together.

Highest waterfall
979 m (3,212 ft)

Tallest geyser
457 m (1,499 ft)

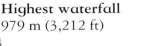

Tallest building
443 m (1,453 ft)

The Angel Falls in Venezuela are twice as high as the world's tallest building.

A geyser in New Zealand shot out water higher than the world's tallest building.

The tallest building is the Sears Tower in Chicago, U.S.A.

Most crowded city

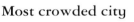

More than 18 million people live in Mexico City – more people than live in the whole of Australia.

Most plants and animals

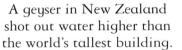

Over half of all plant and animal species live in the rainforests. They are in danger if the forests are destroyed.

Sunniest place

The Sun shines the most in the Sahara Desert in North Africa.

Wettest place

It rains for 350 days every year on Mount Waialeale in the Hawaiian islands.

Coldest place

It is so cold at Vostok in Antarctica that your bare skin would freeze in seconds.

Driest place

Parts of the Atacama Desert in Chile have had no rain for over 400 years.

Glossary

canal
A waterway that is cut through land to join one place to another, so that goods can be carried between them by boat.
(pages 24, 25)

capital city
The most important city of a country. This is where the government of the country passes its laws.
(pages 13, 17, 22, 24, 26, 44, 45)

climate
The pattern of weather throughout the year in each part of the world, such as hot, sunny weather followed by cooler, rainy weather.
(pages 16, 31, 34, 36)

continent
One of seven large areas of land in the world: Africa, Antarctica, Asia, Australia, Europe, North America, and South America.
(pages 10, 11, 18, 38, 40)

crops
Plants that are grown by farmers to provide food for people. Crops are often sold to other countries. Each crop needs the right soil and climate to grow well.
(pages 16, 32, 34, 36)

earthquake
This is caused when large blocks of rock move beneath the surface of the earth. Cracks can open in the ground and buildings may collapse.
(page 22)

Equator
The imaginary line around the Earth, exactly halfway between the North and South Poles. Countries close to the Equator are hot. Countries further away from the Equator are cooler.
(pages 10, 11, 12, 16)

farming
When people use land to grow crops or breed animals for food, or to produce materials such as wool, coffee, rubber, or tobacco.
(pages 17, 24, 25, 28, 29, 32, 34, 35, 36, 38)

fjord
A long, narrow bay or inlet in the rocky coast of Norway.
(page 27)

geyser
A water source, such as a spring, that shoots hot water high up into the air.
(pages 26, 41, 42)

hurricane
A violent storm with very strong winds that can cause a lot of damage to anything in its way.
(page 24)

industry
When goods are made or services are supplied. Different kinds of industry include factories, mines, and banks.
(pages 28, 29, 30)

island
A piece of land that is surrounded on all sides by water. Some islands are very small, such as Nauru; others are very large, such as Greenland.
(pages 18, 19, 22, 24, 30, 31, 37, 40, 41)

mine
A place where natural resources, such as coal, diamonds, or iron ore are dug from the ground.
(pages 28, 29, 38)

monsoon
A season of strong winds and heavy rain in countries around the northern part of the Indian Ocean.
(page 36)

plains
An area of flat, open land with only a few trees. Plains are often covered with grasslands.
(page 22)

port
A town or city on a sea coast with a harbour that is used to transport goods by sea.
(page 24)

prairie
A wide, treeless plain.
(page 20)

province
A particular area or division of a country or state.
(page 17, 21)

state
A large country can be split up into a number of states for administration purposes. For example, Nebraska and Iowa are two of the 50 states that make up the United States of America.
(pages 17, 22, 23)

terrain
An area of land, usually with a particular feature, such as mountains, plains, or rainforest.
(page 16)

territory
Land that belongs to a country or state.
(page 44)

volcano
A mountain or hill that is made up of ash and lava. Lava is hot, liquid rock from inside the Earth, which pours out from a crater when the volcano erupts.
(pages 22, 26, 37)

weather
Rain, wind, snow, fog, and sunshine are all different kinds of weather. Weather forecasts tell people how the weather is likely to change during the day.
(pages 16, 18, 30, 32, 41)

Country index

This index shows the pages on which you can find all the countries and their territories that are shown on the maps in this book. Each country is marked with its capital city.

A

Afghanistan, Kabul 13, 35
Albania, Tirana 13, 31
Algeria, Algiers 13, 38
American Samoa (UNITED STATES OF AMERICA), Pago Pago 12
Andorra, Andorra la Vella 13, 30
Angola, Luanda 13, 39
Anguilla (UNITED KINGDOM), The Valley 12
Antarctica 12, 13, 18
Argentina, Buenos Aires 12, 24, 25
Armenia, Yerevan 13, 32
Ascension (ST HELENA), Georgetown 12
Australia, Canberra 13, 40, 41
Austria, Vienna 13, 28, 29
Azerbaijan, Baku 13, 32

B

Bahamas, Nassau 12, 24
Bahrain, Manamah 13
Bangladesh, Dhaka 13
Barbados, Bridgetown 12, 24
Belgium, Brussels 13, 28
Belize, Belmopan 12, 24
Belorussia, Minsk 13, 32
Benin, Porto-Novo 13, 38
Bermuda (UNITED KINGDOM), Hamilton 12
Bhutan, Thimphu 13, 35
Bolivia, La Paz 12, 25
Bosnia and Herzegovina, Sarajevo 13, 31
Botswana, Gaborone 13, 39
Brazil, Brasilia 12, 25

British Virgin Islands (UNITED KINGDOM), Road Town 12
Brunei, Bandar Seri Begawan 13, 37
Bulgaria, Sofia 13, 31
Burkina, Ouagadougou 12, 38
Burma (Myanmar), Rangoon 13, 35, 36
Burundi, Bujumbura 13, 39

C

Cambodia, Phnom Penh 13, 36
Cameroon, Yaounde 13, 38
Canada, Ottawa 12, 20, 21
Cape Verde, Praia 12
Cayman Islands (UNITED KINGDOM), George Town 24
Central African Republic, Bangui 13, 39
Chad, N'Djamena 13, 39
Chatham Islands (NEW ZEALAND) 12
Chile, Santiago 12, 25
China, Peking (Beijing) 13, 35, 36, 37
Christmas Island (AUSTRALIA) 13
Cocos Islands (AUSTRALIA), West Island 13
Colombia, Bogota 12
Comoros, Moroni 13
Congo, Brazzaville 13, 38, 39
Cook Islands (NEW ZEALAND), Avarua 12
Corsica (FRANCE), Ajaccio 31
Costa Rica, San Jose 12, 24
Croatia, Zagreb 13, 31
Cuba, Havana 12, 24
Cyprus, Nicosia 13, 34
Czech Republic, Prague 13, 29

D

Denmark, Copenhagen 13, 26, 27
Djibouti, Djibouti 13, 39
Dominica, Roseau 12
Dominican Republic, Santo Domingo 12, 24

E

Ecuador, Quito 12, 24, 25
Egypt, Cairo 13, 39
El Salvador, San Salvador 12, 24
Equatorial Guinea, Malabo 13, 38
Eritrea, Asmara 13, 39
Estonia, Tallinn 13, 27
Ethiopia, Addis Ababa 13, 39

F

Faeroe Islands (DENMARK), Torshavn 12, 26
Falkland Islands (UNITED KINGDOM), Stanley 12, 25
Fiji, Suva 13, 41
Finland, Helsinki 13, 26, 27
France, Paris 13, 28, 30
French Guiana (FRANCE), Cayenne 12, 24
French Polynesia (FRANCE), Papeete 12

G

Gabon, Libreville 13, 38
Gambia, Banjul 12, 38
Georgia, Tbilisi 13, 32
Germany, Berlin 13, 28
Ghana, Accra 12, 38
Gibraltar (UNITED KINGDOM), Gibraltar 12
Greece, Athens 13, 31
Greenland (DENMARK), Nuuk 12, 19, 21
Grenada, St George's 12, 24
Guadeloupe (FRANCE), Basse-Terre 12, 24
Guam (UNITED STATES OF AMERICA), Agana 13
Guatemala, Guatemala City 12, 24
Guinea, Conakry 12, 38
Guinea-Bissau, Bissau 12, 38
Guyana, Georgetown 12, 24

H

Haiti, Port-au-Prince 12, 24
Honduras, Tegucigalpa 12, 24
Hong Kong (UNITED KINGDOM), Hong Kong 13, 37
Hungary, Budapest 13, 28, 29

I

Iceland, Reykjavik 12, 26
India, New Delhi 13, 35, 36
Indonesia, Jakarta 13, 37
Iran, Tehran 13, 34
Iraq, Baghdad 13, 34
Ireland, Republic of, Dublin 12, 26
Israel, Jerusalem 13, 34
Italy, Rome 13, 28, 31
Ivory Coast, Yamoussoukro 12, 38

J

Jamaica, Kingston 12, 24
Jan Mayen (NORWAY) 12
Japan, Tokyo 13, 37
Jordan, Amman 13, 34

K

Kazakhstan, Alma Ata 13, 32
Kenya, Nairobi 13, 39
Kiribati, Tarawa 12, 13
Kuwait, Kuwait 13, 34
Kyrgyzstan, Bishkek 13, 32

L

Laos, Vientiane 13, 36
Latvia, Riga 13, 27
Lebanon, Beirut 13, 34
Lesotho, Maseru 13, 39
Liberia, Monrovia 12, 38
Libya, Tripoli 13, 39
Liechtenstein, Vaduz 13, 28
Lithuania, Vilnius 13, 27
Luxembourg, Luxembourg 13, 28

M

Macao (PORTUGAL), Macao 13
Macedonia, Skopje 13, 31
Madagascar, Antananarivo 13, 39
Malawi, Lilongwe 13, 39
Malaysia, Kuala Lumpur 13, 36, 37

ACKNOWLEDGMENTS

Dorling Kindersley would like to thank the following for their assistance in the production of this book:

Cartographic Assistance Tony Chambers
Country Borders Janos Marffy
Design Advice Rowena Alsey
Design Assistance Robin Hunter, Amy McCluskey
Editorial Advice Nicola Tuxworth
Map Type Design Diane Clouting
Picture Assistance Valya Alexander, Miriam Sharland
Signpost Labels Sharon Peters

Thanks also to Trina Wydmanski at Ian Fleming Associates, the agents for Dave Hopkins.

Model Gemmel Cole (photographed by Tim Ridley 14cl)

Photo Agency Credits
a=above; b=bottom or below; c=centre; l=left; r=right; t=top
Bryan and Cherry Alexander 21tl. Christopher Branfield 35tl; / front cover br. Bruce Coleman/Dr Frieder Sauer 34bl. James Davis Travel Photography front cover tcl; / bl. Chris Fairclough Colour Library 29cr; / back cover crb. Greenpeace/Morgan 18cr. Robert Harding Picture Library 19crb; / 36cb: /Bildagentur Schuster/Kummels 24tr, /Bildagentur Schuster/Schmied 24c; /Philip Craven 31tl; /Adam Wolfitt 41crb. The Image Bank/Harald Sund 11bl. Frank Lane Picture Agency/R. Thompson 14bc. Massey Fergusson 20bc. NASA 8bl. Science Photo Library/Tom Van Sant/Geosphere Project/Santa Monica 8/9tc. Spectrum Colour Library front cover cra; / cl. Zefa Picture Library 20cl; / 26clb; / 37c; / 39cr; /F.Damm 22cl; /Deckert 37cra; /Freytag 27cr; /Janicek 32cl.

Chad	Kuwait	South Africa	Cuba	Cameroon
Madagascar	Equatorial Guinea	Congo	Libya	Australia
Swaziland	Surinam	Oman	Vietnam	Algeria
Sri Lanka	Norway	Poland	Malta	Syria
Gabon	Djibouti	Thailand	Switzerland	Ghana
Iran	Grenada	Bolivia	Somalia	Denmark
Ivory Coast	Bahamas	Austria	Botswana	Mozambique